To

FROM_____
_____
_____

DATE_____

WITH THIS SPECIAL MESSAGE

_____
_____
_____
_____

FRIENDS
ARE FRIENDS FOREVER

AND OTHER ENCOURAGEMENTS

FROM GOD'S WORD

WITH PERSPECTIVES BY

MICHAEL W. SMITH

THOMAS NELSON PUBLISHERS
Nashville • Atlanta • London • Vancouver

Text copyright © 1997 by Michael W. Smith

Michael W. Smith's exclusive management by Blanton/Harrell
Entertainment, 2910 Poston Avenue, Nashville, TN 37203.

Photos courtesy of Reunion Records
Photographer Matthew Barnes

Scripture compilation originally published as *God's Promises
for the Graduate*. Copyright © 1989 by Thomas Nelson Publishers.

Published in Nashville, Tennessee, by Thomas Nelson, Inc.

Unless otherwise noted, Scripture quotations are from the
NEW KING JAMES VERSION of the Bible. Copyright ©
1979, 1980, 1982, 1990, 1994, Thomas Nelson, Inc., Publishers.

Scripture quotations noted KJV are from The Holy Bible,
KING JAMES VERSION.

Printed in the United States of America

7 - 03 02 01 00

CONTENTS

A NOTE FROM

MICHAEL W. SMITH

We've probably never met, but I wish we had. Instead of having this book between us, I wish we could kick back in a restaurant and just talk. I'd like to know where you've been and where you think you're going, what has really hurt, what your dreams are, what your thoughts are about God.

Can I tell you right now that I don't want to take anything for granted? Maybe you're graduating with honors or just barely getting that diploma. Maybe you have your life planned down to the smallest detail or have no clue what the future holds. You could be the most popular student on campus or you could feel like the invisible person hardly anyone notices.

Perhaps you got this book because you like my music or came to one of my concerts—or maybe it came as a gift from someone who believes in you with the same conviction that he or she believes in the One who made you. Whether you are totally fired up about your relationship with Christ or you hardly ever think about God, I hope you find something here for you.

I'd like to tell you a few stories from my life—some wrong roads I've traveled, some right decisions I've made, and some ways in which God has often taken my mistakes and turned them to something good.

As you read, I hope you'll see that we're alike in many ways and that we both really need the kind of guidance that comes only from our Father in heaven.

If I were to make a list of my strengths, I guarantee you that public speaking would not be in my Top Ten. But in June 1991, I was invited to give the commencement address at my alma mater, Ceredo-Kenova High School in West Virginia. I'd be the first to admit that I was also not the most impressive student to come from that school, but there I was with an amazing opportunity, fifteen years after graduation, standing before the crowd in my hometown.

After telling some stories on myself—memories cherished, things I had done right, mistakes I had made—I came to what I believe mattered most. Standing before *those eighty-three graduates that day, I told them they were coming to a pivotal point in life. Soon they would be making more decisions for themselves than ever before. None were more important than deciding what they believed about God.*

Was He the God the Bible reveals Him to be, or was it all a clever lie? Walking either path had its ramifications. With my voice echoing across the football field, I quoted Psalm 37:4: "Delight yourself also in the LORD, and He shall give you the desires of your heart."

FIRST "DELIGHT," THEN "DESIRES"

Without a doubt, some of those graduates mentally bypassed the first half of that verse to get to the "desires of your heart." They probably fantasized about owning mansions, jet-setting around the world, and enjoying the lifestyles of the rich and famous. They may realize in time that the "delight" part at the beginning of the verse is really the door that leads to the desires of our hearts. In fact, if we really throw ourselves into enjoying God, He'll even plant the desires that He knows will truly enrich our lives.

When I was in high school, I played piano, but I lived for baseball. I envisioned myself someday in front of cheering crowds, holding a bat, not a microphone. Then when I was fifteen, I didn't make the all-star team. My dream was suddenly crushed. I had no idea that the closing of that door would open another that was far beyond what I could have possibly imagined.

I had become a Christian when I was ten and was active in our family's church, but my involvement increased when my baseball career ended. Every Sunday night I played piano for our praise gatherings. Our youth choir performed incredible musicals, which featured music that was very different from the hymns we sang on Sunday morning. I started listening to artists from the Jesus movement of the early '70s, and I liked what I heard. I "delighted" in the music and the friendships that I found in my youth group. Only looking back years later do I see that God was planting the seeds of desire so that I would grow into my career in music.

Just as Christ told a parable about young plants choked out by weeds, my story could have had a similar ending. As you're about to discover, my journey involved a detour that could have destroyed all that I now cherish. Perhaps you can learn from my mistakes.

DEAD ENDS

After growing up in a loving Christian home, giving my heart to Christ as a boy, and being involved in a great church, I hit the skids my junior year of high school. Some of my closest friends graduated and moved off to college or got married. Without that circle of support, I started hanging out with people who offered me everything I had managed to avoid up to that point. I was testing limits, taking chances, and acting crazy.

When I moved to Nashville in 1978, I sank deeper into that lifestyle. Because I was no longer under the protective eyes of my small-town family and friends, I responded to my newfound freedom with more habits that enslaved me. I kept late hours and wouldn't wake up until afternoon. I was experimenting with drugs and trying to impress people with how cool I was. Instead of acknowledging my musical abilities as a precious gift from God, I took them for granted.

With each step deeper into the mire, I grew more unhappy, more depressed. One night after we had played at a bar, everybody in the band went over to one guy's house to party. There I made a near fatal error by trying a drug that caused an extremely violent reaction. On the way home I thought I was losing my mind. I stayed up all night, terrified about what had happened. I remember praying over and over, "God, don't let me die." The next day I began to recover from the ordeal, but I still didn't take the very large hint to run from that lifestyle.

There was pure wisdom in what Joseph did when Pharaoh's wife made sexual advances. He jumped up and flat out *ran for his life* (Gen. 39:12)! I wasn't so smart, at least not at that point.

During a visit to my parents' home in Kenova, I vividly remember having a quiet but uncomfortable conversation with my father on the porch. With knowing eyes, he softly said, "You're going to have to straighten out your life." He knew that I didn't need a lecture. His few words communicated both the hurt and the love that he felt. Even though I knew my dad was right, I didn't have the faith and self-control to turn from the dead-end alley I was traveling.

A TURNING POINT

In October 1979, I had an experience that I would describe as similar to a minor nervous breakdown. Psalm 38:4–6 paints a pretty accurate picture of what was going on inside me:

For my iniquities have gone over my head;
Like a heavy burden they are too heavy for me.
My wounds are foul and festering
Because of my foolishness.
I am troubled, I am bowed down greatly;
I go mourning all the day long.

The day I hit bottom I was alone in the house. I began to freak out. My thoughts raced. My heart pounded. My body shook. For hours, I lay on the kitchen floor, curled up like a baby.

I can't explain all that was going on inside me, but there came a specific moment when I felt that God joined me there on the floor. He didn't come to condemn me or reprimand me. I already knew that my life was totally out of control. Instead, He came to lift the burden that was crushing me and free me to start again. Inside I knew that God was saying, This is your turning point. *The next day I could sense my life was taking a new direction.*

A BETTER WAY

Although things have not been all blue skies and rain-bows since those reckless years, I've come to recognize that God's ways are far better than mine. Just as my life turned from self-destruction, God started to give me glimpses of what lay in store if I would just delight myself in Him:

For I know the thoughts that I think toward you, says the LORD, thoughts of peace and not of evil, to give you a future and a hope. Then you will call upon Me and go and pray to Me, and I will listen to you. And you will seek Me and find Me, when you seek Me with all your heart. I will be found by you, says the LORD, and I will bring you back from your captivity. *(JER. 29:11–14)*

The LORD really did bring me back from being captive—from being cool and acting in total rebellion—to doing what I knew to be right.

Don't deceive yourself by thinking that you are too strong or smart to stumble. At fifteen, I would have said there was no way I would ever place myself in some of the situations that grew far too familiar. Sin will take you farther, keep you longer, and cost you more than you can ever see at the outset.

Right now, are you a prisoner to anything? Resist the temptation to quickly answer "No!" and read on, because I don't want you to speed beyond something so important. Are you trapped by your image, your ego, or your pride? Have you been covering up an addiction to pornography, clothes, or food? Do you have a clean slate before God with sexuality? Are there people you refuse to forgive? Is it easy to excuse jealousy or rage?

If you are being held captive, Christ offers the key to your freedom. He said, "Whoever commits sin is a slave of sin. And a slave does not abide in the house forever, but a son abides forever. Therefore if the Son makes you free, you shall be free indeed" (John 8:34–36).

Start by confessing that sin to God. Then if you have wronged other people, do everything in your power to make it right. If you need to have someone pray for you to help you get rid of the guilt and shame, find someone trustworthy and come clean.

Not only will the Son make you free, but His Father has promised to give you a future and a hope.

In my travels, I've met people who feel stuck, believing that their lives will never change for the better. They think that today is the same as yesterday and tomorrow will be no better. To borrow a song title from Steven Curtis Chapman, there really is "more to this life."

MORE TO THIS LIFE

Whether you're in high school or college, you're preparing to write the next chapter of your life. Can you sense if seeds have been planted in you? How ready do you feel? What's going to give structure to what lies ahead?

With all my heart, I believe that God's Word will give more insight on who you are and how to live than any class or seminar you will attend, any training program you will complete, or any textbook you will read. I know a man whose Bible has the words Manufacturer's Handbook *tooled into its leather cover. You may think that's a little corny, but it's true. Who could possibly know more about life than the One who created it?*

God's Word has truly been a part of my career. When I find myself really in tune with Him and His Word, songs often come out. Sometimes I sit at the piano to read my Bible. As I think about the verses, I may mess around with chord progressions. Occasionally, a melody forms, based on the passages I've been reading.

In fact, King David and the writers of the New Testament have been some of my favorite collaborators over the years. Back in 1981, Sandi Patty gave my writing career a huge boost by recording "How Majestic Is Your Name."

The music was mine, but the words were straight out of Psalm 8.

On my first album, many of the song ideas were sparked by something that my wife, Debbie, and I were reading in the Bible or the pastor was preaching at church. "Great Is the Lord" was borrowed from Psalm 48:1. "Be Strong and Courageous" was inspired by God's charge to Joshua (Josh. 1). "Love in the Light" came from 1 John 1:7. "The Race Is On" was shaped from the scene described in Hebrews 12:1–3.

Probably more than anyone else, Don Finto, my pastor and friend for more than fifteen years, has made Scripture come alive to me. When you have a conversation with him, Scripture just flows out. He isn't trying to impress you or sound spiritual or educated—it's just a part of him.

Debbie grew up in Nashville so she sounds southern (which, by the way, I love). I don't think she could eliminate traces of that drawl if she lived in Brooklyn the rest of her life. When she talks, that southern accent just comes out in her words. In the same way, Don so immerses himself in Scripture—reading it, meditating on it, memorizing it—that it just comes out when he speaks.

You may think this makes sense for a pastor, but question its relevance for your life. Yet stop a moment and re-

member a time you faced questions whose answers seemed beyond you. Recalling Bible verses filed into your heart will give more direction than you might initially suspect.

Let's say a raunchy TV show comes on. What do you do? A verse pops into your mind: "I will set nothing wicked before my eyes" (Ps. 101:3). Your friends try to convince you to violate morals, and you remember:

> **Blessed is the man**
> **Who walks not in the counsel of the ungodly,**
> **Nor stands in the path of sinners,**
> **Nor sits in the seat of the scornful. (Ps. 1:1)**

You're tempted to stress out over a situation, and the Holy Spirit reminds you:

> **"Be anxious for nothing, but in everything by prayer and supplication, with thanksgiving, let your requests be made known to God; and the peace of God, which surpasses all understanding, will guard your hearts and minds through Christ Jesus" (Phil. 4:6–7).**

Just as I found myself without solid Christian friends to help me remain strong after high school, you can easily become isolated from the truth if you don't look to the Scriptures. I've found that they have led me to accomplish way beyond what I could hope or imagine.

BEYOND WHAT YOU CAN HOPE OR IMAGINE

Right now my older son, Ryan, is into movies in a big way. He and his buddies are writing screenplays, making videos, and using computer software that allows you to act as a director and editor. (He may become the Steven Spielberg of his generation, and maybe he'll hire his dad to score the sound track!) Whether he stays with those interests or leaps into something totally different, one thing I know: God promises to give him a future and a hope.

Just as clay can be shaped in many ways by the potter's skillful hands, you have no idea what God may have in store for you. Often, God does the unexpected to show that all good gifts really do have their origin in Him (Matt. 7:11).

That was certainly the case with the song "Friends." Back in 1982, Debbie and I rented a little duplex on the west side of Nashville. Every Sunday night a roomful of people would come together for Bible study and worship. When Bill Jackson, a good friend and member of our group, announced that he was taking a position with

Campus Crusade in Auburn, we were all deeply saddened.

Two hours before the last Bible study he was going to be with us, Debbie dropped a bombshell on me. "We need to do something for Bill," she said. "Let's write a song for him."

Suddenly taking the role of the pragmatist, I responded, "But, Deb, that's two hours from now. How are we going to write a song before the meeting?" I dismissed the idea and went out to play with our dog.

Fifteen minutes later, she approached me with a sheet of paper. On it were the lyrics that I have now sung hundreds, maybe thousands, of times. I went to the piano, and in five minutes the song was completed. When we sang it for Bill that night, there were plenty of tears to go around.

Since that time, plenty more tears have been shed while that song has played. I have received mailboxes full of letters that tell how that song has been used at camps, funerals, and, of course, graduations.

It's certainly not the catchiest melody I've composed and the words aren't the finest poetry that Debbie has written, but "Friends" has probably touched more lives in more ways than anything I've ever done. Just as Christ used the basics—fish and bread—to ultimately feed a crowd of five thousand, God has taken this simple little song and made it into something meaningful.

As you pack up for what lies ahead, I pray that the Lord will direct each step of your journey through life. I know with all my heart that amazing things await you if you truly delight in the Lord.

THE BASIS FOR
GOD'S PROMISES

M ost of my recording these days takes place at my Deer Valley studio in Franklin, Tennessee, or various facilities that are just minutes away from fast-food restaurants there. However, working on an album at Caribou Ranch is like experiencing life on the frontier. Nestled in the majestic Rocky Mountains, the dozen or so rustic buildings are surrounded by literally thousands of acres of virgin forest.

My first recording experience at Caribou Ranch was playing keyboards for Amy Grant's Straight Ahead album in 1983. It was like being at summer camp because we would eat our meals together and work in the studio, then head into the mountains when we needed some down-time.

Late one night after we finished recording, Amy began to walk back to her cabin alone, but it was so dark, she got lost in the woods. (Remembering that we had talked about bears earlier that evening probably didn't make her feel calmer about the situation!) After stumbling around a bit, she saw a very faint light off in the distance and decided to walk toward it.

Eventually, she realized that it was her porch light. Relieved to be safe and sound, she sat down and pulled out a cassette tape that had a song I had begun. The melody was finished, but I didn't have verses—just a chorus taken from Psalm 119:105: "Thy word is a lamp unto my feet, and a light unto my path" (KJV). Reflecting on her unnerving experience, Amy combined her thoughts with Scripture to write verses that portrayed the struggles we often face.

Like her, we can stumble around in the dark, fearful of a bear lurking behind the next tree, or we can look for a light to guide us. With all my heart, I believe that the Bible illuminates our paths.

HIDING GOD'S WORD
IN YOUR HEART

Some years ago, my pastor challenged me to begin memorizing Scripture. Honestly, I had never really done much of that, other than John 3:16 and "Jesus wept," but I had witnessed the impact of memorized Scripture on some of my friends. I started with the first chapter of Colossians, which paints a vivid picture of who Christ is, and then I worked on Psalm 139.

After I had committed it to memory, I began quoting the psalm at concerts on the "Friends" tour in 1985, and you could hear a pin drop every time. Over the years, we've invested a ton of money in sophisticated lighting effects, elaborate stage designs, and even a grand piano that levitated on a hydraulic system, but nothing I've ever done from a stage has generated more positive comments than when I would walk around the stage and simply quote that psalm.

If you've never tried to memorize Scripture, Psalm 139 is a great starting place because it is filled with so many wonderful truths. It begins: "O LORD, You have searched me and known me."

Boom! What a mind-blowing concept to think that the Creator of the universe knows you intimately—what makes you tick, your strengths, your weaknesses, your potential!

Verses 9–10 say,

> *If I take the wings of the morning,*
> *And dwell in the uttermost parts of the sea,*
> *Even there Your hand shall lead me,*
> *And Your right hand shall hold me.*

Depending on the nature of your relationship with God, that could be an unbelievable comfort or an irritating nuisance. If you want Him right beside you, that's a promise that you're never alone. If, however, you think you can slip something by without God's knowing it, think again. Is God there to annoy you? No, He sees what will harm you and what will move you forward on life's journey. You can save yourself a ton of heartache by holding tightly to the hand that wants to lead you home.

Maybe my favorite section of Psalm 139 is verses 17–18:

> *How precious also are Your thoughts to me,*
> *O God!*
> *How great is the sum of them!*
> *If I should count them, they would be more*
> *in number than the sand.*

That God is spending a lot of time thinking about you.

If I had to write a thesis statement for Psalm 139, it

would probably go something like this: God knows you far better than you know yourself, and He considers you with great affection.

GOD IS THINKING ABOUT YOU

Ask about my five kids, and you'll get a rundown on how each is unique. Ryan is a walking encyclopedia on movie special effects. Whitney loves playing piano. Emily is a fanatic about horses. Tyler goes crazy playing drums, just as I did as a boy. Anna likes to play ball, especially if Dad is pitching.

They're all Smiths, but each is an individual. Disciplining one child might be as simple as saying, "Don't do that." Another one might require consequences for his or her actions. God knows just what it takes to correct you and just what it takes to invigorate you. Why? Because He knows you so well and His thoughts about you would outnumber the grains of sand on the broadest beach you've ever walked.

Is God a "heavenly monitor"? I can honestly say that He has never taken anything away from me that was good for me. Has He blocked my path when I was bent on selfishness or gratifying some impure appetite? Yes. Has He let me suffer consequences when I stubbornly refused to heed His warnings? Definitely.

I love a line from C. S. Lewis's book The Lion, the Witch, and the Wardrobe. *While visiting with Mr. and Mrs. Beaver, a young girl named Lucy inquires about a lion known as Aslan, who symbolizes Christ.* " 'Course he isn't safe. But he's good," *replies Mr. Beaver. That's Christ—good but not always safe.*

In one sense, going along with the crowd is the safe thing to do. It requires no energy, no backbone, no guts. Taking up your cross to follow Jesus isn't safe; truly living for Him means putting your life on the line.

Years ago, I went rappelling for the first time. Someone tied me into a harness, and then came the moment of truth. I had to lean backward over the edge of the cliff, trusting the rope to hold.

In truth, I didn't have the rope—it had me. (At least, I hoped it did!) The first time I rappelled, I didn't really feel all that safe, but the experience felt good. It was a thrill, hanging over the cliff, bouncing off the side of the rocky mountainside, lowering myself to the ground one hundred feet below.

I wonder if some who question God's intentions for their lives are like those who stand on the cliff, never willing to experience God's holding their lives in His good and capable hands.

Far from being a wet blanket, the Lord wants to see us

living in joy beyond our wildest imagination. Jesus even gave this as a mission statement: "I have come that they may have life, and that they may have it more abundantly" (John 10:10).

ABUNDANT LIVING

Not long ago, I had the opportunity to play some of my songs with the Nashville Symphony Orchestra in front of fourteen thousand people. What a rush! Even though that was a huge thrill, it is just one slice of the abundant life that God offers me. Watching my daughter Anna dancing around our house wearing several of her ballerina outfits at once is a total joy, but it too is just one more slice.

Second Corinthians 1:20 declares "For all the promises of God in Him are Yes." Doesn't that make you a little curious about what He has promised? Most of the pages in this book are filled with just that—God's promises to you, covering a wide range of topics ranging from faith to forgiveness, loneliness to fellowship, discouragement to perseverance.

He has said Yes to us in Christ and awaits our response. Look into His Word, discover what He is saying, and say Yes to Him. May the Scriptures be a lamp unto our feet and a light unto our paths.

THE BASIS FOR GOD'S PROMISES

THE BIBLE—THE MANUFACTURER'S HANDBOOK

All Scripture is given by inspiration of God, and is profitable for doctrine, for reproof, for correction, for instruction in righteousness, that the man of God may be complete, thoroughly equipped for every good work.

2 TIMOTHY 3:16–17

You search the Scriptures, for in them you think you have eternal life; and these are they which testify of Me.

JOHN 5:39

Knowing this first, that no prophecy of Scripture is of any private interpretation, for prophecy never came by the will of man, but holy men of God spoke as they were moved by the Holy Spirit.

2 PETER 1:20–21

Therefore whoever hears these sayings of Mine, and does them, I will liken him to a wise man who built his house on the rock: and the rain descended, the floods came, and the winds blew and beat on that house; and it did not fall, for it was founded on the rock.

MATTHEW 7:24–25

Most assuredly, I say to you, he who hears My word and believes in Him who sent Me has everlasting life, and shall not come into judgment, but has passed from death into life.

JOHN 5:24

Every word of God is pure;
He is a shield to those who put their trust in Him.
Do not add to His words,
Lest He rebuke you, and you be found a liar.

PROVERBS 30:5–6

By the word of the LORD the heavens were
    made,
And all the host of them by the breath of His
    mouth.

PSALM 33:6

For the word of God is living and powerful, and sharper than any two-edged sword, piercing even to the division of soul and spirit, and of joints and marrow, and is a discerner of the thoughts and intents of the heart.

HEBREWS 4:12

Let all the earth fear the LORD;
Let all the inhabitants of the world stand in awe of
    Him.
For He spoke, and it was done;
He commanded, and it stood fast.

PSALM 33:8–9

For I testify to everyone who hears the words of the
prophecy of this book: If anyone adds to these
things, God will add to him the plagues that are
written in this book; and if anyone takes away from
the words of the book of this prophecy, God shall
take away his part from the Book of Life, from the
holy city, and from the things which are written in
this book.

REVELATION 22:18–19

Heaven and earth will pass away, but My words will
by no means pass away.

MARK 13:31

For as the rain comes down, and the snow from
    heaven,
And do not return there,
But water the earth,
And make it bring forth and bud,
That it may give seed to the sower
And bread to the eater,
So shall My word be that goes forth from My
    mouth;

It shall not return to Me void,
But it shall accomplish what I please,
And it shall prosper in the thing for which I sent it.

ISAIAH 55:10–11

Blessed be the LORD, who has given rest to His
people Israel, according to all that He promised.
There has not failed one word of all His good
promise, which He promised through His servant
Moses.

1 KINGS 8:56

My son, give attention to my words;
Incline your ear to my sayings.
Do not let them depart from your eyes;
Keep them in the midst of your heart;
For they are life to those who find them,
And health to all their flesh.

PROVERBS 4:20–22

THE BIBLE—OUR COMFORT

For whatever things were written before were written
for our learning, that we through the patience and
comfort of the Scriptures might have hope.

ROMANS 15:4

And these things we write to you that your joy may
be full.

1 JOHN 1:4

My son, do not forget my law,
But let your heart keep my commands;
For length of days and long life
And peace they will add to you.

PROVERBS 3:1–2

But as it is written:
"Eye has not seen, nor ear heard,
Nor have entered into the heart of man
The things which God has prepared for those who
love Him."

1 CORINTHIANS 2:9

My son, give attention to my words;
Incline your ear to my sayings.
Do not let them depart from your eyes;
Keep them in the midst of your heart;
For they are life to those who find them,
And health to all their flesh.

PROVERBS 4:20–22

This is my comfort in my affliction,
For Your word has given me life.

PSALM 119:50

Unless Your law had been my delight,
I would then have perished in my affliction.

PSALM 119:92

So then faith comes by hearing, and hearing by the word of God.

ROMANS 10:17

The law of the LORD is perfect, converting the
  soul;
The testimony of the LORD is sure, making wise
  the simple;
The statutes of the LORD are right, rejoicing the
  heart;
The commandment of the LORD is pure,
  enlightening the eyes;

PSALM 19:7–8

Therefore lay aside all filthiness and overflow of wickedness, and receive with meekness the implanted word, which is able to save your souls. . . . But he who looks into the perfect law of liberty and continues in it, and is not a forgetful hearer but a doer of the work, this one will be blessed in what he does.

JAMES 1:21, 25

Great peace have those who love Your law,
And nothing causes them to stumble.

PSALM 119:165

If you keep My commandments, you will abide in My love, just as I have kept My Father's commandments and abide in His love. These

things I have spoken to you, that My joy may
remain in you, and that your joy may be full.

JOHN 15:10–11

And if you are Christ's, then you are Abraham's
seed, and heirs according to the promise.

GALATIANS 3:29

In My Father's house are many mansions; if it were
not so, I would have told you. I go to prepare a
place for you. And if I go and prepare a place for
you, I will come again and receive you to Myself;
that where I am, there you may be also.

JOHN 14:2–3

Then the King will say to those on His right hand,
"Come, you blessed of My Father, inherit the
kingdom prepared for you from the foundation of
the world."

MATTHEW 25:34

Now to Him who is able to keep you from
stumbling,
And to present you faultless
Before the presence of His glory with exceeding joy,
To God our Savior,
Who alone is wise,
Be glory and majesty, dominion and power,
Both now and forever.
Amen.

JUDE 24–25

Every word of God is pure;
He is a shield to those who put their trust in Him.

PROVERBS 30:5

THE BIBLE—OUR GUIDE

This Book of the Law shall not depart from your
mouth, but you shall meditate in it day and night,
that you may observe to do according to all that is
written in it. For then you will make your way
prosperous, and then you will have good success.

JOSHUA 1:8

Then Jesus said to those Jews who believed Him,
"If you abide in My word, you are My disciples
indeed. And you shall know the truth, and the
truth shall make you free."

JOHN 8:31–32

All Scripture is given by inspiration of God, and is
profitable for doctrine, for reproof, for correction,
for instruction in righteousness, that the man of
God may be complete, thoroughly equipped for
every good work.

2 TIMOTHY 3:16–17

When you roam, they will lead you;
When you sleep, they will keep you;
And when you awake, they will speak with you.
For the commandment is a lamp,

And the law a light;
Reproofs of instruction are the way of life.

PROVERBS 6:22–23

Your word is a lamp to my feet
And a light to my path.

PSALM 119:105

Trust in the LORD with all your heart,
And lean not on your own understanding;
In all your ways acknowledge Him,
And He shall direct your paths.

PROVERBS 3:5–6

The law of the LORD is perfect, converting the
    soul;
The testimony of the LORD is sure, making wise
    the simple.

PSALM 19:7

Your ears shall hear a word behind you, saying,
"This is the way, walk in it,"
Whenever you turn to the right hand
Or whenever you turn to the left.

ISAIAH 30:21

How can a young man cleanse his way?
By taking heed according to Your word.

PSALM 119:9

Your word I have hidden in my heart,
That I might not sin against You.

PSALM 119:11

As He spoke by the mouth of His holy prophets,
Who have been since the world began.

LUKE 1:70

To give light to those who sit in darkness and the
    shadow of death,
To guide our feet into the way of peace.

LUKE 1:79

Your testimonies also are my delight
And my counselors.

PSALM 119:24

If any of you lacks wisdom, let him ask of God,
who gives to all liberally and without reproach, and
it will be given to him.

JAMES 1:5

I will instruct you and teach you in the way you
    should go;
I will guide you with My eye.

PSALM 32:8

For You are my lamp, O LORD;
The LORD shall enlighten my darkness.

2 SAMUEL 22:29

For You are my rock and my fortress;
Therefore, for Your name's sake,
Lead me and guide me.

PSALM 31:3

THE BIBLE—OUR STRENGTH

Having been born again, not of corruptible seed
but incorruptible, through the word of God which
lives and abides forever.

1 PETER 1:23

So now, brethren, I commend you to God and to
the word of His grace, which is able to build you
up and give you an inheritance among all those
who are sanctified.

ACTS 20:32

Now He who establishes us with you in Christ and
has anointed us is God, who also has sealed us and
given us the Spirit in our hearts as a guarantee.

2 CORINTHIANS 1:21–22

All flesh is as grass,
And all the glory of man as the flower of the grass.
The grass withers,
And its flower falls away,
But the word of the LORD endures forever.

1 PETER 1:24–25

Blessed be the LORD, who has given rest to His people Israel, according to all that He promised. There has not failed one word of all His good promise, which He promised through His servant Moses.

1 KINGS 8:56

The counsel of the LORD stands forever,
The plans of His heart to all generations.

PSALM 33:11

The works of His hands are verity and justice;
All His precepts are sure.
They stand fast forever and ever,
And are done in truth and uprightness.

PSALM 111:7–8

Forever, O LORD,
Your word is settled in heaven.

PSALM 119:89

In Him you also trusted, after you heard the word of truth, the gospel of your salvation; in whom also, having believed, you were sealed with the Holy Spirit of promise, who is the guarantee of our inheritance until the redemption of the purchased possession, to the praise of His glory.

EPHESIANS 1:13–14

As for God, His way is perfect;
The word of the LORD is proven;
He is a shield to all who trust in Him.

PSALM 18:30

The eternal God is your refuge,
And underneath are the everlasting arms;
He will thrust out the enemy from before you,
And will say, "Destroy!"

DEUTERONOMY 33:27

For thus says the Lord GOD, the Holy One of
Israel:
"In returning and rest you shall be saved;
In quietness and confidence shall be your
strength."
But you would not.

ISAIAH 30:15

My soul melts from heaviness;
Strengthen me according to Your word.

PSALM 119:28

But those who wait on the LORD
Shall renew their strength;
They shall mount up with wings like eagles,
They shall run and not be weary,
They shall walk and not faint.

ISAIAH 40:31

~No~ CONDEMNATION

PROMISES OF SALVATION

O ccasionally, someone asks me if I have a favorite Bible verse. Although many have special meaning to me, the single most powerful remains Romans 8:1: "There is therefore now no condemnation to those who are in Christ Jesus."

Now that's good news! If you're like me, you can really get down on yourself. Sometimes I find myself thinking, I can't believe I was so stupid. Or, Man, I really blew it here. In times like these, I don't need anybody to kick me around because I'm doing such a good job on my own.

Right in the middle of that deepening darkness, a light comes on. A voice whispers, No condemnation. I'm embarrassed to admit that I've argued against that truth knocking on my heart. Yeah, but what about . . . ? I'll respond. Sometimes we just don't feel good enough.

NEVER GOOD ENOUGH

I get all kinds of letters from all kinds of people. Some are from fans thanking me for my music, and many are from people who are really struggling in some way.

Often a letter will say something like this: "I can never be good enough for God." (Unfortunately, some churches promote this thinking, causing people to feel terrible about themselves because they can never measure up.)

That's not what God says of anyone. Instead take a glimpse at how He looks at us, according to Psalm 103:10–12:

> He has not dealt with us according to our sins,
> Nor punished us according to our iniquities.
> For as the heavens are high above the earth,
> So great is His mercy toward those who fear Him;
> As far as the east is from the west,
> So far has He removed our trangressions from us.

Allow me to provide my own brief paraphrase: God is nuts about us. This psalm goes on to say that God has compassion for us the way that a father has compassion for his children. That analogy is powerful to a dad like me.

THOUGHTS FROM A FATHER

I am crazy about my kids, but sometimes they do things that try my patience. Yet even in their worst moments of tantrum throwing or stubbornness, I still love them. When they feel left out by their classmates or fail in something they try, it really wears me out too. Over the past few years, God has been calling me to be a better father, but I know that my level of compassion does not approach how much He cares for us.

Although you may have heard this verse a hundred times, its truth is as potent as ever: "For God so loved the world that He gave His only begotten Son, that whoever believes in Him should not perish but have everlasting life" (John 3:16). That's compassion in its purest form— sacrificing His own Son to reconcile us to Himself.

I'm thinking about a young girl who is perishing right now. She has become obsessed with physical perfection. For her, that means being thin. Her mom is terrified as she watches her precious daughter starving herself, a victim of anorexia. My wife, Debbie, struggled with the disease when she was in high school so she knows exactly how powerful the pull can be. She has tried to encourage this girl and her mom by exposing the lie of pursuing physical perfection and reinforcing how much God loves her as she is.

How will the girl escape this brutal trap of unrelenting self-control? Eating will help restore her physically, but that is only a part of the solution. She must become convinced that she was made in the image of a tender and compassionate God who loves her so much He grieves to see her lose pound after pound until her bones become all too apparent. She must begin to see herself as a person valued by God and worthy of love. She must learn to release her clenched fist of control to the One who made her in His own image.

Maybe you have a hard time being fully convinced of God's love for other reasons. Maybe your family has come apart. Maybe you've been abused in some way. I know of a man whose childhood was marked by violence and verbal abuse from an alcoholic father. But if you talk to him, he won't tell you that God ripped him off by having him grow up in such an environment.

Instead, he will say that God prepared him to love anyone in need of comfort and understanding. And he will tell you that growing up as he did uniquely qualified him to work in foreign missions where chaos is the normal working environment. He believes that God really can cause all things to work out for good (Rom. 8:28), but sometimes it takes years for that truth to be realized.

BEFORE AND AFTER

Maybe you've done something that you know was wrong, but you just can't put it behind you. First Corinthians 6:9–11 reads like a list of society's least desirable people: adulterers, idolaters, thieves, drunkards, slanderers, and swindlers. Not the kind of people you would want for your roommates. Then comes the payoff: "And such were some of you. But you were washed, but you were sanctified, but you were justified in the name of the Lord Jesus and by the Spirit of our God."

This letter was written to members of the early church. It reminds them of their former lives and then tells the rest of the story.

And it speaks to us today, saying, "It doesn't matter what you're doing or what you've done. God's salvation is bigger than the worst mess you can create for yourself."

When you decide to walk away from your foolishness, God's response is always "No condemnation." True, you may live with the consequences of your actions, and scars may remain long after the wounds have been healed, but God will not hold grudges. Remember His Word promises, "As far as the east is from the west, / So far has He removed our transgressions from us."

Take a moment in silence. Listen to what God wants to tell you as many times as it takes until it penetrates your heart. No condemnation. No condemnation. No condemnation.

PROMISES OF SALVATION

THE NEED FOR SALVATION

The Lord is not slack concerning His promise, as some count slackness, but is longsuffering toward us, not willing that any should perish but that all should come to repentance.

2 PETER 3:9

What then? Are we better than they? Not at all. For we have previously charged both Jews and Greeks that they are all under sin.

As it is written:
"There is none righteous, no, not one;
There is none who understands;
There is none who seeks after God.

They have all turned aside;
They have together become unprofitable;
There is none who does good, no, not one."

ROMANS 3:9–12

Jesus answered and said to him, "Most assuredly, I say to you, unless one is born again, he cannot see the kingdom of God."

JOHN 3:3

Truly, these times of ignorance God overlooked, but now commands all men everywhere to repent, because He has appointed a day on which He will judge the world in righteousness by the Man whom He has ordained. He has given assurance of this to all by raising Him from the dead.

ACTS 17:30–31

For all have sinned and fall short of the glory of God.

ROMANS 3:23

And in them the prophecy of Isaiah is fulfilled, which says:
    "Hearing you will hear and shall not understand,
    And seeing you will see and not perceive;
    For the hearts of this people have grown dull.
    Their ears are hard of hearing,
    And their eyes they have closed,

Lest they should see with their eyes and hear
    with their ears,
Lest they should understand with their hearts
    and turn,
So that I should heal them."

MATTHEW 13:14–15

For the wages of sin is death, but the gift of God is
eternal life in Christ Jesus our Lord.

ROMANS 6:23

But in accordance with your hardness and your
impenitent heart you are treasuring up for yourself
wrath in the day of wrath and revelation of the
righteous judgment of God.

ROMANS 2:5

For to be carnally minded is death, but to be
spiritually minded is life and peace. Because the
carnal mind is enmity against God; for it is not
subject to the law of God, nor indeed can be. So
then, those who are in the flesh cannot please God.

ROMANS 8:6–8

There is a way that seems right to a man,
But its end is the way of death.

PROVERBS 14:12

O wretched man that I am! Who will deliver me
from this body of death? I thank God—through

Jesus Christ our Lord! So then, with the mind I myself serve the law of God, but with the flesh the law of sin.

ROMANS 7:24–25

Let no one deceive you with empty words, for because of these things the wrath of God comes upon the sons of disobedience.

EPHESIANS 5:6

Therefore put to death your members which are on the earth: fornication, uncleanness, passion, evil desire, and covetousness, which is idolatry. Because of these things the wrath of God is coming upon the sons of disobedience.

COLOSSIANS 3:5–6

THE PROVISION OF SALVATION

For God so loved the world that He gave His only begotten Son, that whoever believes in Him should not perish but have everlasting life.

JOHN 3:16

In Him we have redemption through His blood, the forgiveness of sins, according to the riches of His grace.

EPHESIANS 1:7

For God did not send His Son into the world to condemn the world, but that the world through Him might be saved.

JOHN 3:17

For the Son of Man has come to seek and to save that which was lost.

LUKE 19:10

Him God has exalted to His right hand to be Prince and Savior, to give repentance to Israel and forgiveness of sins.

ACTS 5:31

For I delivered to you first of all that which I also received: that Christ died for our sins according to the Scriptures.

1 CORINTHIANS 15:3

For when we were still without strength, in due time Christ died for the ungodly. For scarcely for a righteous man will one die; yet perhaps for a good man someone would even dare to die. But God demonstrates His own love toward us, in that while we were still sinners, Christ died for us.

ROMANS 5:6–8

And we know that the Son of God has come and has given us an understanding, that we may know Him who is true; and we are in Him who is true, in

His Son Jesus Christ. This is the true God and eternal life.

1 JOHN 5:20

For it is the God who commanded light to shine out of darkness, who has shone in our hearts to give the light of the knowledge of the glory of God in the face of Jesus Christ.

2 CORINTHIANS 4:6

For if when we were enemies we were reconciled to God through the death of His Son, much more, having been reconciled, we shall be saved by His life.

ROMANS 5:10

And she will bring forth a Son, and you shall call His name JESUS, for He will save His people from their sins.

MATTHEW 1:21

THE GRACE OF GOD

Not by works of righteousness which we have done, but according to His mercy He saved us, through the washing of regeneration and renewing of the Holy Spirit.

TITUS 3:5

For by grace you have been saved through faith, and that not of yourselves; it is the gift of God.

EPHESIANS 2:8

Who has saved us and called us with a holy calling, not according to our works, but according to His own purpose and grace which was given to us in Christ Jesus before time began.

2 TIMOTHY 1:9

To the praise of the glory of His grace, by which He has made us accepted in the Beloved.

EPHESIANS 1:6

Let us therefore come boldly to the throne of grace, that we may obtain mercy and find grace to help in time of need.

HEBREWS 4:16

Then I will give them a heart to know Me, that I am the LORD; and they shall be My people, and I will be their God, for they shall return to Me with their whole heart.

JEREMIAH 24:7

For sin shall not have dominion over you, for you are not under law but under grace.

ROMANS 6:14

But we believe that through the grace of the Lord Jesus Christ we shall be saved in the same manner as they.

ACTS 15:11

But the free gift is not like the offense. For if by the one man's offense many died, much more the grace of God and the gift by the grace of the one Man, Jesus Christ, abounded to many.

ROMANS 5:15

CONVICTION

The sacrifices of God are a broken spirit,
A broken and a contrite heart—
These, O God, You will not despise.

PSALM 51:17

Nevertheless I tell you the truth. It is to your advantage that I go away; for if I do not go away, the Helper will not come to you; but if I depart, I will send Him to you. And when He has come, He will convict the world of sin, and of righteousness, and of judgment: of sin, because they do not believe in Me; of righteousness, because I go to My Father and you see Me no more; of judgment, because the ruler of this world is judged.

JOHN 16:7–11

Who show the work of the law written in their hearts, their conscience also bearing witness, and between themselves their thoughts accusing or else excusing them.

ROMANS 2:15

Now when they heard this, they were cut to the heart, and said to Peter and the rest of the apostles, "Men and brethren, what shall we do?"

ACTS 2:37

For I acknowledge my transgressions,
And my sin is always before me.
Against You, You only, have I sinned,
And done this evil in Your sight—
That You may be found just when You speak,
And blameless when You judge.

PSALM 51:3–4

See, O LORD, that I am in distress;
My soul is troubled;
My heart is overturned within me,
For I have been very rebellious.
Outside the sword bereaves,
At home it is like death.

LAMENTATIONS 1:20

Then he called for a light, ran in, and fell down trembling before Paul and Silas. And he brought them out and said, "Sirs, what must I do to be saved?"

ACTS 16:29–30

Then call, and I will answer;
Or let me speak, then You respond to me.

How many are my iniquities and sins?
Make me know my transgression and my sin.

JOB 13:22–23

Then they said to one another, "We are truly guilty concerning our brother, for we saw the anguish of his soul when he pleaded with us, and we would not hear; therefore this distress has come upon us." And Reuben answered them, saying, "Did I not speak to you, saying, 'Do not sin against the boy'; and you would not listen? Therefore behold, his blood is now required of us."

GENESIS 42:21–22

FAITH

For by grace you have been saved through faith, and that not of yourselves; it is the gift of God.

EPHESIANS 2:8

So they said, "Believe on the Lord Jesus Christ, and you will be saved, you and your household."

ACTS 16:31

He who believes and is baptized will be saved; but he who does not believe will be condemned.

MARK 16:16

That if you confess with your mouth the Lord Jesus and believe in your heart that God has raised

Him from the dead, you will be saved. For with the heart one believes unto righteousness, and with the mouth confession is made unto salvation.

ROMANS 10:9–10

To Him all the prophets witness that, through His name, whoever believes in Him will receive remission of sins.

ACTS 10:43

But without faith it is impossible to please Him, for he who comes to God must believe that He is, and that He is a rewarder of those who diligently seek Him.

HEBREWS 11:6

Jesus said to her, "I am the resurrection and the life. He who believes in Me, though he may die, he shall live."

JOHN 11:25

Then He said to the woman, "Your faith has saved you. Go in peace."

LUKE 7:50

Believe Me that I am in the Father and the Father in Me, or else believe Me for the sake of the works themselves. Most assuredly, I say to you, he who believes in Me, the works that I do he will do also;

and greater works than these he will do, because I
go to My Father.

JOHN 14:11–12

The centurion answered and said, "Lord, I am not
worthy that You should come under my roof. But
only speak a word, and my servant will be healed.
For I also am a man under authority, having
soldiers under me. And I say to this one, 'Go,' and
he goes; and to another, 'Come,' and he comes; and
to my servant, 'Do this,' and he does it." When
Jesus heard it, He marveled, and said to those who
followed, "Assuredly, I say to you, I have not found
such great faith, not even in Israel!"

MATTHEW 8:8–10

Then he said to Jesus, "Lord, remember me when
You come into Your kingdom." And Jesus said to
him, "Assuredly, I say to you, today you will be
with Me in Paradise."

LUKE 23:42–43

For to you it has been granted on behalf of Christ,
not only to believe in Him, but also to suffer for
His sake.

PHILIPPIANS 1:29

REPENTANCE

Then Peter said to them, "Repent, and let every one of you be baptized in the name of Jesus Christ for the remission of sins; and you shall receive the gift of the Holy Spirit. For the promise is to you and to your children, and to all who are afar off, as many as the Lord our God will call."

ACTS 2:38–39

I have not come to call the righteous, but sinners, to repentance.

LUKE 5:32

Or do you despise the riches of His goodness, forbearance, and longsuffering, not knowing that the goodness of God leads you to repentance?

ROMANS 2:4

If we say that we have no sin, we deceive ourselves, and the truth is not in us. If we confess our sins, He is faithful and just to forgive us our sins and to cleanse us from all unrighteousness.

1 JOHN 1:8–9

Repent therefore and be converted, that your sins may be blotted out, so that times of refreshing may come from the presence of the Lord.

ACTS 3:19

Draw near to God and He will draw near to you.
Cleanse your hands, you sinners; and purify your
hearts, you double-minded. Lament and mourn
and weep! Let your laughter be turned to mourning
and your joy to gloom. Humble yourselves in the
sight of the Lord, and He will lift you up.

JAMES 4:8–10

And it shall come to pass
That whoever calls on the name of the LORD
Shall be saved.

ACTS 2:21

Repent, for the kingdom of heaven is at hand!

MATTHEW 3:2

For you were like sheep going astray, but have now
returned to the Shepherd and Overseer of your
souls.

1 PETER 2:25

Now I rejoice, not that you were made sorry, but
that your sorrow led to repentance. For you were
made sorry in a godly manner, that you might
suffer loss from us in nothing.

2 CORINTHIANS 7:9

Seek good and not evil,
That you may live;

So the LORD God of hosts will be with you,
As you have spoken.

AMOS 5:14

CONFESSION

That if you confess with your mouth the Lord
Jesus and believe in your heart that God has raised
Him from the dead, you will be saved. For with the
heart one believes unto righteousness, and with the
mouth confession is made unto salvation.

ROMANS 10:9–10

Therefore whoever confesses Me before men, him I
will also confess before My Father who is in heaven.

MATTHEW 10:32

Confess your trespasses to one another, and pray
for one another, that you may be healed. The
effective, fervent prayer of a righteous man avails
much.

JAMES 5:16

If we confess our sins, He is faithful and just to
forgive us our sins and to cleanse us from all
unrighteousness.

1 JOHN 1:9

I acknowledged my sin to You,
And my iniquity I have not hidden.

I said, "I will confess my transgressions to the
   LORD,"
And You forgave the iniquity of my sin. Selah

PSALM 32:5

Let us hold fast the confession of our hope without
wavering, for He who promised is faithful.

HEBREWS 10:23

Deliver me from the guilt of bloodshed, O God,
The God of my salvation,
And my tongue shall sing aloud of Your
   righteousness.
O LORD, open my lips,
And my mouth shall show forth Your praise.

PSALM 51:14–15

While, through the proof of this ministry, they
glorify God for the obedience of your confession to
the gospel of Christ, and for your liberal sharing
with them and all men.

2 CORINTHIANS 9:13

Also I say to you, whoever confesses Me before
men, him the Son of Man also will confess before
the angels of God.

LUKE 12:8

Then all the land of Judea, and those from Jerusalem, went out to him and were all baptized by him in the Jordan River, confessing their sins.

MARK 1:5

Therefore I make known to you that no one speaking by the Spirit of God calls Jesus accursed, and no one can say that Jesus is Lord except by the Holy Spirit.

1 CORINTHIANS 12:3

And that every tongue should confess that Jesus Christ is Lord, to the glory of God the Father.

PHILIPPIANS 2:11

You have put gladness in my heart,
More than in the season that their grain and wine
    increased.

PSALM 4:7

Yet I will rejoice in the LORD,
I will joy in the God of my salvation.

HABAKKUK 3:18

ACCEPTANCE

All that the Father gives Me will come to Me, and the one who comes to Me I will by no means cast out.

JOHN 6:37

"Come now, and let us reason together,"
Says the LORD,
"Though your sins are like scarlet,
They shall be as white as snow;
Though they are red like crimson,
They shall be as wool."

ISAIAH 1:18

I will cleanse them from all their iniquity by which
they have sinned against Me, and I will pardon all
their iniquities by which they have sinned and by
which they have transgressed against Me.

JEREMIAH 33:8

For the Scripture says, "Whoever believes on Him
will not be put to shame."

ROMANS 10:11

Much more then, having now been justified by His
blood, we shall be saved from wrath through Him.
For if when we were enemies we were reconciled to
God through the death of His Son, much more,
having been reconciled, we shall be saved by His
life.

ROMANS 5:9–10

Now all things are of God, who has reconciled us
to Himself through Jesus Christ, and has given us
the ministry of reconciliation, that is, that God was

in Christ reconciling the world to Himself, not imputing their trespasses to them, and has committed to us the word of reconciliation.

2 CORINTHIANS 5:18–19

But when the wicked turns from his wickedness and does what is lawful and right, he shall live because of it.

EZEKIEL 33:19

Coming to Him as to a living stone, rejected indeed by men, but chosen by God and precious, you also, as living stones, are being built up a spiritual house, a holy priesthood, to offer up spiritual sacrifices acceptable to God through Jesus Christ.

1 PETER 2:4–5

I, even I, am He who blots out your transgressions
    for My own sake;
And I will not remember your sins.

ISAIAH 43:25

"Therefore I say to you, her sins, which are many, are forgiven, for she loved much. But to whom little is forgiven, the same loves little." Then He said to her, "Your sins are forgiven."

LUKE 7:47–48

Bless the LORD, O my soul;
And all that is within me, bless His holy name!
Bless the LORD, O my soul,
And forget not all His benefits:
Who forgives all your iniquities,
Who heals all your diseases,
Who redeems your life from destruction,
Who crowns you with lovingkindness and tender
    mercies,
Who satisfies your mouth with good things,
So that your youth is renewed like the eagle's.

PSALM 103:1–5

As far as the east is from the west,
So far has He removed our transgressions from us.
As a father pities his children,
So the LORD pities those who fear Him.

PSALM 103:12–13

For God did not appoint us to wrath, but to obtain
salvation through our Lord Jesus Christ, who died
for us, that whether we wake or sleep, we should
live together with Him.

1 THESSALONIANS 5:9–10

JUSTIFICATION

Blessed is he whose transgression is forgiven,
Whose sin is covered.

Blessed is the man to whom the LORD does not
  impute iniquity,
And in whose spirit there is no deceit.

PSALM 32:1–2

That having been justified by His grace we should
become heirs according to the hope of eternal life.

TITUS 3:7

Therefore, having been justified by faith, we have
peace with God through our Lord Jesus Christ.

ROMANS 5:1

And by Him everyone who believes is justified
from all things from which you could not be
justified by the law of Moses.

ACTS 13:39

For I will be merciful to their unrighteousness, and
their sins and their lawless deeds I will remember
no more.

HEBREWS 8:12

And the inhabitant will not say, "I am sick";
The people who dwell in it will be forgiven their
iniquity.

ISAIAH 33:24

You see then that a man is justified by works, and
not by faith only. Likewise, was not Rahab the

harlot also justified by works when she received the messengers and sent them out another way? For as the body without the spirit is dead, so faith without works is dead also.

JAMES 2:24–26

There is therefore now no condemnation to those who are in Christ Jesus, who do not walk according to the flesh, but according to the Spirit. . . . Who shall bring a charge against God's elect? It is God who justifies. Who is he who condemns? It is Christ who died, and furthermore is also risen, who is even at the right hand of God, who also makes intercession for us.

ROMANS 8:1, 33–34

Knowing that a man is not justified by the works of the law but by faith in Jesus Christ, even we have believed in Christ Jesus, that we might be justified by faith in Christ and not by the works of the law; for by the works of the law no flesh shall be justified.

GALATIANS 2:16

Then He adds, "Their sins and their lawless deeds I will remember no more." Now where there is remission of these, there is no longer an offering for sin.

HEBREWS 10:17–18

In the LORD all the descendants of Israel
Shall be justified, and shall glory.

ISAIAH 45:25

Therefore the law was our tutor to bring us to
Christ, that we might be justified by faith.

GALATIANS 3:24

RIGHTEOUSNESS

For He made Him who knew no sin to be sin for
us, that we might become the righteousness of God
in Him.

2 CORINTHIANS 5:21

Yet indeed I also count all things loss for the
excellence of the knowledge of Christ Jesus my
Lord, for whom I have suffered the loss of all
things, and count them as rubbish, that I may gain
Christ and be found in Him, not having my own
righteousness, which is from the law, but that
which is through faith in Christ, the righteousness
which is from God by faith.

PHILIPPIANS 3:8–9

For I am not ashamed of the gospel of Christ, for it
is the power of God to salvation for everyone who
believes, for the Jew first and also for the Greek.
For in it the righteousness of God is revealed from

faith to faith; as it is written, "The just shall live by faith."

ROMANS 1:16–17

And he believed in the LORD, and He accounted it to him for righteousness.

GENESIS 15:6

But seek first the kingdom of God and His righteousness, and all these things shall be added to you.

MATTHEW 6:33

Listen to Me, you stubborn-hearted,
Who are far from righteousness:
I bring My righteousness near, it shall not be far
     off;
My salvation shall not linger.
And I will place salvation in Zion,
For Israel My glory.

ISAIAH 46:12–13

Stand therefore, having girded your waist with truth, having put on the breastplate of righteousness.

EPHESIANS 6:14

In Your name they rejoice all day long,
And in Your righteousness they are exalted.

PSALM 89:16

When Christ who is our life appears, then you also will appear with Him in glory. Therefore put to death your members which are on the earth: fornication, uncleanness, passion, evil desire, and covetousness, which is idolatry.

COLOSSIANS 3:4–5

For the grace of God that brings salvation has appeared to all men, teaching us that, denying ungodliness and worldly lusts, we should live soberly, righteously, and godly in the present age, looking for the blessed hope and glorious appearing of our great God and Savior Jesus Christ.

TITUS 2:11–13

As obedient children, not conforming yourselves to the former lusts, as in your ignorance; but as He who called you is holy, you also be holy in all your conduct, because it is written, "Be holy, for I am holy."

1 PETER 1:14–16

DELIVERANCE

O wretched man that I am! Who will deliver me from this body of death? I thank God—through Jesus Christ our Lord! So then, with the mind I myself serve the law of God, but with the flesh the law of sin.

ROMANS 7:24–25

Grace to you and peace from God the Father and our Lord Jesus Christ, who gave Himself for our sins, that He might deliver us from this present evil age, according to the will of our God and Father.

GALATIANS 1:3–4

The angel of the LORD encamps all around those
    who fear Him,
And delivers them.

PSALM 34:7

And you shall know the truth, and the truth shall make you free.

JOHN 8:32

"For the eyes of the LORD are on the righteous,
And His ears are open to their prayers;
But the face of the LORD is against those who do
    evil."
And who is he who will harm you if you become
    followers of what is good?

1 PETER 3:12–13

But the Lord is faithful, who will establish you and guard you from the evil one.

2 THESSALONIANS 3:3

But know that the LORD has set apart for Himself
    him who is godly;
The LORD will hear when I call to Him.

PSALM 4:3

He shall deliver you in six troubles,
Yes, in seven no evil shall touch you.

JOB 5:19

Then the Lord knows how to deliver the godly out
of temptations and to reserve the unjust under
punishment for the day of judgment.

2 PETER 2:9

He who believes in Him is not condemned; but he
who does not believe is condemned already, because
he has not believed in the name of the only
begotten Son of God.

JOHN 3:18

No temptation has overtaken you except such as is
common to man; but God is faithful, who will not
allow you to be tempted beyond what you are able,
but with the temptation will also make the way of
escape, that you may be able to bear it.

1 CORINTHIANS 10:13

Wait on the LORD;
Be of good courage,
And He shall strengthen your heart;
Wait, I say, on the LORD!

PSALM 27:14

For You, O LORD, will bless the righteous;
With favor You will surround him as with a shield.

PSALM 5:12

And He said to me, "My grace is sufficient for you,
for My strength is made perfect in weakness."
Therefore most gladly I will rather boast in my
infirmities, that the power of Christ may rest upon
me.

2 CORINTHIANS 12:9

For in that He Himself has suffered, being
tempted, He is able to aid those who are tempted.

HEBREWS 2:18

You are of God, little children, and have overcome
them, because He who is in you is greater than he
who is in the world.

1 JOHN 4:4

ADOPTION

For as many as are led by the Spirit of God, these
are sons of God. For you did not receive the spirit
of bondage again to fear, but you received the
Spirit of adoption by whom we cry out, "Abba,
Father."

ROMANS 8:14–15

For you are all sons of God through faith in Christ
Jesus.

GALATIANS 3:26

Having predestined us to adoption as sons by Jesus
Christ to Himself, according to the good pleasure
of His will.

EPHESIANS 1:5

Behold what manner of love the Father has
bestowed on us, that we should be called children
of God! Therefore the world does not know us,
because it did not know Him. Beloved, now we are
children of God; and it has not yet been revealed
what we shall be, but we know that when He is
revealed, we shall be like Him, for we shall see Him
as He is.

1 JOHN 3:1–2

But as many as received Him, to them He gave the
right to become children of God, to those who
believe in His name.

JOHN 1:12

But when the fullness of the time had come, God
sent forth His Son, born of a woman, born under
the law, to redeem those who were under the law,
that we might receive the adoption as sons.

GALATIANS 4:4–5

Now, therefore, you are no longer strangers and foreigners, but fellow citizens with the saints and members of the household of God . . . in whom you also are being built together for a dwelling place of God in the Spirit.

EPHESIANS 2:19, 22

I will be a Father to you,
And you shall be My sons and daughters,
Says the LORD Almighty.

2 CORINTHIANS 6:18

For whoever does the will of My Father in heaven is My brother and sister and mother.

MATTHEW 12:50

For both He who sanctifies and those who are being sanctified are all of one, for which reason He is not ashamed to call them brethren.

HEBREWS 2:11

"For whom the LORD loves He chastens,
And scourges every son whom He receives."
If you endure chastening, God deals with you as with sons; for what son is there whom a father does not chasten?

HEBREWS 12:6–7

PERSEVERANCE

And we desire that each one of you show the same diligence to the full assurance of hope until the end, that you do not become sluggish, but imitate those who through faith and patience inherit the promises.

HEBREWS 6:11–12

For whatever is born of God overcomes the world. And this is the victory that has overcome the world— our faith. Who is he who overcomes the world, but he who believes that Jesus is the Son of God?

1 JOHN 5:4–5

For he who lacks these things is shortsighted, even to blindness, and has forgotten that he was cleansed from his old sins. Therefore, brethren, be even more diligent to make your call and election sure, for if you do these things you will never stumble.

2 PETER 1:9–10

Therefore do not cast away your confidence, which has great reward. For you have need of endurance, so that after you have done the will of God, you may receive the promise.

HEBREWS 10:35–36

He who overcomes shall be clothed in white garments, and I will not blot out his name from the

Book of Life; but I will confess his name before My Father and before His angels.

REVELATION 3:5

As you therefore have received Christ Jesus the Lord, so walk in Him, rooted and built up in Him and established in the faith, as you have been taught, abounding in it with thanksgiving.

COLOSSIANS 2:6–7

Let us hold fast the confession of our hope without wavering, for He who promised is faithful. And let us consider one another in order to stir up love and good works.

HEBREWS 10:23–24

I do not pray that You should take them out of the world, but that You should keep them from the evil one.

JOHN 17:15

Therefore submit to God. Resist the devil and he will flee from you.

JAMES 4:7

Then the Lord knows how to deliver the godly out of temptations and to reserve the unjust under punishment for the day of judgment.

2 PETER 2:9

For if we sin willfully after we have received the knowledge of the truth, there no longer remains a sacrifice for sins, but a certain fearful expectation of judgment, and fiery indignation which will devour the adversaries.

HEBREWS 10:26–27

Be of good courage,
And He shall strengthen your heart,
All you who hope in the LORD.

PSALM 31:24

"So I will strengthen them in the LORD,
And they shall walk up and down in His name,"
Says the LORD.

ZECHARIAH 10:12

Strengthen the weak hands,
And make firm the feeble knees.
Say to those who are fearful-hearted,
"Be strong, do not fear!
Behold, your God will come with vengeance,
With the recompense of God;
He will come and save you."

ISAIAH 35:3–4

GUIDANCE

However, when He, the Spirit of truth, has come, He will guide you into all truth; for He will not

speak on His own authority, but whatever He hears
He will speak; and He will tell you things to come.

JOHN 16:13

The steps of a good man are ordered by the
  LORD,
And He delights in his way.

PSALM 37:23

And I will pray the Father, and He will give you
another Helper, that He may abide with you
forever.

JOHN 14:16

I will not leave you orphans; I will come to you.

JOHN 14:18

For He shall give His angels charge over you,
To keep you in all your ways.
In their hands they shall bear you up,
Lest you dash your foot against a stone.

PSALM 91:11–12

I say then: Walk in the Spirit, and you shall not
fulfill the lust of the flesh.

GALATIANS 5:16

I have seen his ways, and will heal him;
I will also lead him,

And restore comforts to him
And to his mourners.

ISAIAH 57:18

You will guide me with Your counsel,
And afterward receive me to glory.

PSALM 73:24

For He instructs him in right judgment,
His God teaches him.

ISAIAH 28:26

A man's heart plans his way,
But the LORD directs his steps.

PROVERBS 16:9

Indeed He would have brought you out of dire
distress.

JOB 36:16

Then they cried out to the LORD in their trouble,
And He saved them out of their distresses.

PSALM 107:19

For a righteous man may fall seven times
And rise again,
But the wicked shall fall by calamity.

PROVERBS 24:16

The righteous is delivered from trouble,
And it comes to the wicked instead.

PROVERBS 11:8

PROMISES FOR
SPIRITUAL GROWTH

F ew people realize how dangerous success can be. Failure can be unbelievably painful, but it always keeps you humble. Success can build your ego, make you arrogant and demanding, destroy your relationships, and ultimately leave your soul poorer than failure ever will.

Back in 1985, I was riding high on the enthusiastic response to my album The Big Picture. A mainstream label expressed interest in releasing one of the songs to pop radio stations. Visions of being on the charts alongside Elton John or Billy Joel danced in my head. It was going to be a dream come true, and I got all pumped up about it.

In short, it didn't happen, and I took the news really

hard. I felt disappointed, rejected, angry. In retrospect, I can see that God prevented it because He knew I wasn't ready.

Several albums later, the song "Place in This World" from the album Go West, Young Man *began getting airplay on pop stations. Instead of being cocky about it, I was genuinely humbled.*

I'll never forget the first time I heard this song on a pop station. I was driving south on I-65 from Nashville toward my home in Franklin when 106 FM played it. I was so overcome, I had to pull off the road. I just sat there crying.

"Place in This World" wasn't a sentimental love song. It asked people to seriously think about their lives. I was blown away to have the opportunity to tell people that God wants to show them the place He has for them. I remember sitting in the car thinking about how many people were listening to this song that Amy Grant, Wayne Kirkpatrick, and I had written about God. For the first time, I wasn't just "preaching to the choir," although I'm grateful for the support I've received on Christian radio stations. With this song, anyone could have been listening—and was.

WORTH IT ALL

Soon after "Place in This World" became a hit, I received a letter from a woman who made the controversy of getting mainstream airplay worthwhile. She was separated from her husband, she said, and struggling in her relationships with her two children. She was so low, she was contemplating suicide. One day she heard this song on a pop station, and it spoke to her heart.

After weeping over her need to find guidance from God, she accepted Christ and eventually reconciled with her family. My song had been the catalyst for all those changes, she told me. Of course, I wasn't responsible for that impact in her life; the Holy Spirit used the lyrics of this song to draw her to God.

When you're in sync with God, you can accept a compliment, but remember that the real thanks belong to Him. I'm famous around my house for making French toast, but I let my kids in on the production even though they sometimes make a big mess. God is the same way; He lets us help, although sometimes we don't necessarily handle things as neatly as He would. All too often we're too busy searching for security, which interferes with our spiritual growth.

THE SEARCH FOR SECURITY

Because "Place in This World" was very successful, I found myself in the company of some pretty powerful people. I realized that many based their worth upon the clout they carried, their fame, their wealth. Without God alive in their lives, some were pretty sad and empty.

Just as Christ presented in His parable, they were building their lives on sand. Ultimately, the storms come and everything can get washed away. In His story, rain falls on the wise man as well, but only he had the sense to build on rock that would withstand any storm.

So how can you stormproof your life? No matter what you see on the news or at the movies, security is not found in how many dollars you've got in the bank, how big a house you live in, or how prosperous your career is. All these things are fleeting—here today and gone tomorrow.

Isaiah 40:8 puts it this way: "The grass withers, the flower fades, / But the word of our God stands forever." Try as you might, you won't find a way to cheat the system, to create your own immortality.

Unfortunately, all of us fall prey to the trap of success and adulation. I will never forget finishing a concert in Seattle on The Big Picture tour. The crowd had been absolutely amazing, and I was stoked when we walked off *after playing the last song of the set. I was standing back-stage, taking it all in. People were screaming for an en-core, and I have to admit I was loving the response. A few members of the audience up in the balcony had managed to get where they could see me waiting behind the curtain. They were repeatedly screaming, "We love you, Michael!"*

I waved to them, which made them yell even louder. I started thinking, This is great!

Suddenly, I felt a warm, heavy hand on my shoulder. It was my pastor, Don Finto. His clear blue eyes told me he could see right through me. I was caught. "Give it up. Just give it up. It's not you," he said, leaning close to be heard above the cheering crowd.

Immediately, I felt an unbelievable conviction that my ego was out of control. I said, "You're right. It's not me."

If there's anything good in me, it's because Christ has placed it there. He gets the credit. Only He is due the honor and the glory. If I get it, it will wither just like the grass in my yard.

Yet our society judges almost everything in tangible terms—records sold, dollars earned, the kind of car you drive. But the eye can see only so much. Sometimes unseen forces interfere with our spiritual growth.

WHAT YOUR EYES CAN'T

On my I 2 Eye *album, I recorded an instrumental called "Ashton," named for the fictional town in Frank Peretti's book* This Present Darkness. *Something in his storytelling captured my imagination and forced me to think about spiritual warfare as never before.*

That exact term isn't in the Bible, but we see examples of it there. The basics are simple: two forces are at work in our world—good and evil, God and Satan. According to John 10:10, the devil's job description is to steal, kill, and destroy. In the prophetic writing of Isaiah 61:1–3, Christ's mission is radically different:

> *The Spirit of the Lord GOD is upon Me,*
> *Because the LORD has anointed Me*
> *To preach good tidings to the poor;*
> *He has sent Me to heal the brokenhearted . . .*
> *To comfort all who mourn,*
> *To console those who mourn in Zion,*
> *To give them beauty for ashes,*
> *The oil of joy for mourning,*
> *The garment of praise for the spirit of heaviness;*
> *That they may be called trees of righteousness,*
> *The planting of the LORD, that He may be glorified.*

In Peretti's book, the angels of heaven clash with demons over control of people's lives as the town of Ashton becomes a spiritual battlefield. Prayer is the primary weapon in the Christians' arsenal. When they cry out to God, the enemy forces are pushed back.

Now I won't say that it is always as simple as that or that we are always aware of such conflicts, but I believe that our human eyes will never capture all the forces at work around us.

GROWING UP

To be ready for the battle that we face every day, we've got to grow up and get beyond our pettiness and pride: "Be strong in the Lord and in the power of His might. Put on the whole armor of God, that you may be able to stand against the wiles of the devil" (Eph. 6:10–11).

Imagine how boring it would be to spend the rest of our lives in kindergarten. Likewise, we're meant to expand our knowledge, mature in our thinking, deepen our capacity to serve, and sink our roots farther into the living waters of God that nourish our souls.

Let's look up, grow up, and reach up to the calling He has given us.

PROMISES FOR SPIRITUAL GROWTH

IN FAITH AND TRUST

For whatever is born of God overcomes the world. And this is the victory that has overcome the world—our faith.

1 JOHN 5:4

That the genuineness of your faith, being much more precious than gold that perishes, though it is tested by fire, may be found to praise, honor, and glory at the revelation of Jesus Christ, whom having not seen you love. Though now you do not see Him, yet believing, you rejoice with joy inexpressible and full of glory, receiving the end of your faith—the salvation of your souls.

1 PETER 1:7–9

So then faith comes by hearing, and hearing by the word of God.

ROMANS 10:17

Looking unto Jesus, the author and finisher of our faith, who for the joy that was set before Him endured the cross, despising the shame, and has sat down at the right hand of the throne of God.

HEBREWS 12:2

"For the eyes of the LORD are on the righteous,
And His ears are open to their prayers;
But the face of the LORD is against those who do
    evil."
And who is he who will harm you if you become
    followers of what is good?

1 PETER 3:12–13

For in it the righteousness of God is revealed from faith to faith; as it is written, "The just shall live by faith."

ROMANS 1:17

For we walk by faith, not by sight.

2 CORINTHIANS 5:7

But without faith it is impossible to please Him, for he who comes to God must believe that He is, and that He is a rewarder of those who diligently seek Him.

HEBREWS 11:6

I say, through the grace given to me, to everyone who is among you, not to think of himself more highly than he ought to think, but to think soberly, as God has dealt to each one a measure of faith.

ROMANS 12:3

Now faith is the substance of things hoped for, the evidence of things not seen.

HEBREWS 11:1

Yet the righteous will hold to his way,
And he who has clean hands will be stronger and
    stronger.

JOB 17:9

Knowing that the testing of your faith produces patience.

JAMES 1:3

Blessed is the man who endures temptation; for when he has been approved, he will receive the crown of life which the Lord has promised to those who love Him.

JAMES 1:12

When you pass through the waters, I will be with
    you;
And through the rivers, they shall not overflow you.
When you walk through the fire, you shall not be
    burned,
Nor shall the flame scorch you.

ISAIAH 43:2

For the eyes of the LORD run to and fro throughout the whole earth, to show Himself strong on behalf of those whose heart is loyal to Him. In this you have done foolishly; therefore from now on you shall have wars.

2 CHRONICLES 16:9

But the Lord is faithful, who will establish you and guard you from the evil one.

2 THESSALONIANS 3:3

IN LOVE OF GOD

And we know that all things work together for good to those who love God, to those who are the called according to His purpose.

ROMANS 8:28

He who has My commandments and keeps them, it is he who loves Me. And he who loves Me will be loved by My Father, and I will love him and manifest Myself to him.

JOHN 14:21

Listen, my beloved brethren: Has God not chosen the poor of this world to be rich in faith and heirs of the kingdom which He promised to those who love Him?

JAMES 2:5

But as it is written:

"Eye has not seen, nor ear heard,
Nor have entered into the heart of man
The things which God has prepared for those who
   love Him."

1 CORINTHIANS 2:9

In this love, not that we loved God, but that He
loved us and sent His Son to be the propitiation for
our sins. Beloved, if God so loved us, we also ought
to love one another. . . . And we have known and
believed the love that God has for us. God is love,
and he who abides in love abides in God, and God
in him. . . . We love Him because He first loved us.

1 JOHN 4:10–11, 16, 19

But if anyone loves God, this one is known by Him.

1 CORINTHIANS 8:3

And I said: "I pray, LORD God of heaven, O great
and awesome God, You who keep Your covenant
and mercy with those who love You and observe
Your commandments."

NEHEMIAH 1:5

For the Father Himself loves you, because you have
loved Me, and have believed that I came forth from
God.

JOHN 16:27

IN LOVE OF OTHERS

Beloved, if God so loved us, we also ought to love one another. No one has seen God at any time. If we love one another, God abides in us, and His love has been perfected in us.

1 JOHN 4:11–12

Finally, all of you be of one mind, having compassion for one another; love as brothers, be tenderhearted, be courteous; not returning evil for evil or reviling for reviling, but on the contrary blessing, knowing that you were called to this, that you may inherit a blessing.

1 PETER 3:8–9

This is My commandment, that you love one another as I have loved you. Greater love has no one than this, than to lay down one's life for his friends.

JOHN 15:12–13

"And you shall love the LORD your God with all your heart, with all your soul, with all your mind, and with all your strength." This is the first commandment. And the second, like it, is this: "You shall love your neighbor as yourself." There is no other commandment greater than these.

MARK 12:30–31

Though I speak with the tongues of men and of angels, but have not love, I have become sounding brass or a clanging cymbal. And though I have the gift of prophecy, and understand all mysteries and all knowledge, and though I have all faith, so that I could remove mountains, but have not love, I am nothing. And though I bestow all my goods to feed the poor, and though I give my body to be burned, but have not love, it profits me nothing. Love suffers long and is kind; love does not envy; love does not parade itself, is not puffed up; does not behave rudely, does not seek its own, is not provoked, thinks no evil; does not rejoice in iniquity, but rejoices in the truth; bears all things, believes all things, hopes all things, endures all things. Love never fails. But whether there are prophecies, they will fail; whether there are tongues, they will cease; whether there is knowledge, it will vanish away.

1 CORINTHIANS 13:1–8

By this all will know that you are My disciples, if you have love for one another.

JOHN 13:35

But I say to you, love your enemies, bless those who curse you, do good to those who hate you, and pray for those who spitefully use you and persecute you.

MATTHEW 5:44

And this commandment we have from Him: that he who loves God must love his brother also.

1 JOHN 4:21

Beloved, do not avenge yourselves, but rather give place to wrath; for it is written, "Vengeance is Mine, I will repay," says the Lord. Therefore
"If your enemy is hungry, feed him;
If he is thirsty, give him a drink;
For in so doing you will heap coals of fire on his head."
Do not be overcome by evil, but overcome evil with good.

ROMANS 12:19–21

Since you have purified your souls in obeying the truth through the Spirit in sincere love of the brethren, love one another fervently with a pure heart.

1 PETER 1:22

Beloved, let us love one another, for love is of God; and everyone who loves is born of God and knows God. He who does not love does not know God, for God is love.

1 JOHN 4:7–8

He who loves his brother abides in the light, and there is no cause for stumbling in him.

1 JOHN 2:10

But do not forget to do good and to share, for with such sacrifices God is well pleased.

HEBREWS 13:16

Behold, how good and how pleasant it is
For brethren to dwell together in unity!
It is like the precious oil upon the head,
Running down on the beard,
The beard of Aaron,
Running down on the edge of his garments.

PSALM 133:1–2

We know that we have passed from death to life, because we love the brethren. He who does not love his brother abides in death. . . . My little children, let us not love in word or in tongue, but in deed and in truth. And by this we know that we are of the truth, and shall assure our hearts before Him.

1 JOHN 3:14, 18–19

For God is not unjust to forget your work and labor of love which you have shown toward His name, in that you have ministered to the saints, and do minister.

HEBREWS 6:10

Finally, brethren, farewell. Become complete. Be of good comfort, be of one mind, live in peace; and the God of love and peace will be with you.

2 CORINTHIANS 13:11

IN PEACE

Be anxious for nothing, but in everything by prayer and supplication, with thanksgiving, let your requests be made known to God; and the peace of God, which surpasses all understanding, will guard your hearts and minds through Christ Jesus.

PHILIPPIANS 4:6–7

Therefore, having been justified by faith, we have peace with God through our Lord Jesus Christ.

ROMANS 5:1

Peace I leave with you, My peace I give to you; not as the world gives do I give to you. Let not your heart be troubled, neither let it be afraid.

JOHN 14:27

For to be carnally minded is death, but to be spiritually minded is life and peace.

ROMANS 8:6

You will keep him in perfect peace,
Whose mind is stayed on You,
Because he trusts in You.

ISAIAH 26:3

Great peace have those who love Your law,
And nothing causes them to stumble.

PSALM 119:165

Finally, brethren, farewell. Become complete. Be of good comfort, be of one mind, live in peace; and the God of love and peace will be with you.

2 CORINTHIANS 13:11

LORD, You will establish peace for us,
For You have also done all our works in us.

ISAIAH 26:12

Mark the blameless man, and observe the upright;
For the future of that man is peace.

PSALM 37:37

For you shall go out with joy,
And be led out with peace;
The mountains and the hills
Shall break forth into singing before you,
And all the trees of the field shall clap their hands.

ISAIAH 55:12

For the kingdom of God is not eating and drinking, but righteousness and peace and joy in the Holy Spirit. For he who serves Christ in these things is acceptable to God and approved by men. Therefore let us pursue the things which make for peace and the things by which one may edify another.

ROMANS 14:17–19

The work of righteousness will be peace,
And the effect of righteousness, quietness and
    assurance forever.

ISAIAH 32:17

Now may the Lord of peace Himself give you
peace always in every way. The Lord be with you
all.

2 THESSALONIANS 3:16

And let the peace of God rule in your hearts, to
which also you were called in one body; and be
thankful.

COLOSSIANS 3:15

Now may the God of hope fill you with all joy and
peace in believing, that you may abound in hope by
the power of the Holy Spirit.

ROMANS 15:13

All your children shall be taught by the LORD,
And great shall be the peace of your children.

ISAIAH 54:13

But now in Christ Jesus you who once were far off
have been brought near by the blood of Christ. For
He Himself is our peace, who has made both one,
and has broken down the middle wall of
separation.

EPHESIANS 2:13–14

IN MATURITY

However, when He, the Spirit of truth, has come,
He will guide you into all truth; for He will not
speak on His own authority, but whatever He hears
He will speak; and He will tell you things to come.

JOHN 16:13

If you seek her as silver,
And search for her as for hidden treasures;
Then you will understand the fear of the LORD,
And find the knowledge of God.
For the LORD gives wisdom;
From His mouth come knowledge and
    understanding;
He stores up sound wisdom for the upright;
He is a shield to those who walk uprightly.

PROVERBS 2:4–7

Now we have received, not the spirit of the world,
but the Spirit who is from God, that we might
know the things that have been freely given to us
by God.

1 CORINTHIANS 2:12

Evil men do not understand justice,
But those who seek the LORD understand all.

PROVERBS 28:5

But of Him you are in Christ Jesus, who became for us wisdom from God—and righteousness and sanctification and redemption.

1 CORINTHIANS 1:30

For I will give you a mouth and wisdom which all your adversaries will not be able to contradict or resist.

LUKE 21:15

Being confident of this very thing, that He who has begun a good work in you will complete it until the day of Jesus Christ.

PHILIPPIANS 1:6

Now may the God of peace Himself sanctify you completely; and may your whole spirit, soul, and body be preserved blameless at the coming of our Lord Jesus Christ. He who calls you is faithful, who also will do it.

1 THESSALONIANS 5:23–24

Then Jesus spoke to them again, saying, "I am the light of the world. He who follows Me shall not walk in darkness, but have the light of life."

JOHN 8:12

The fear of the LORD is the beginning of wisdom;
A good understanding have all those who do His
  commandments.
His praise endures forever.

PSALM 111:10

I will bring the blind by a way they did not know;
I will lead them in paths they have not known.
I will make darkness light before them,
And crooked places straight.
These things I will do for them,
And not forsake them.

ISAIAH 42:16

With Him are wisdom and strength,
He has counsel and understanding.

JOB 12:13

I say then: Walk in the Spirit, and you shall not
fulfill the lust of the flesh.

GALATIANS 5:16

For if these things are yours and abound, you will
be neither barren nor unfruitful in the knowledge
of our Lord Jesus Christ.

2 PETER 1:8

He shall be like a tree
Planted by the rivers of water,
That brings forth its fruit in its season,

Whose leaf also shall not wither;
And whatever he does shall prosper.

PSALM 1:3

Every branch in Me that does not bear fruit He takes away; and every branch that bears fruit He prunes, that it may bear more fruit. . . . I am the vine, you are the branches. He who abides in Me, and I in him, bears much fruit; for without Me you can do nothing.

JOHN 15:2, 5

IN FORGIVING OTHERS

And whenever you stand praying, if you have anything against anyone, forgive him, that your Father in heaven may also forgive you your trespasses.

MARK 11:25

Then Peter came to Him and said, "Lord, how often shall my brother sin against me, and I forgive him? Up to seven times?" Jesus said to him, "I do not say to you, up to seven times, but up to seventy times seven."

MATTHEW 18:21–22

Bearing with one another, and forgiving one another, if anyone has a complaint against another; even as Christ forgave you, so you also must do.

COLOSSIANS 3:13

For if you forgive men their trespasses, your heavenly Father will also forgive you. But if you do not forgive men their trespasses, neither will your Father forgive your trespasses.

MATTHEW 6:14–15

Therefore
  "If your enemy is hungry, feed him;
  If he is thirsty, give him a drink;
  For in so doing you will heap coals of fire on his head."
  Do not be overcome by evil, but overcome evil with good.

ROMANS 12:20–21

But I say to you, love your enemies, bless those who curse you, do good to those who hate you, and pray for those who spitefully use you and persecute you, that you may be sons of your Father in heaven; for He makes His sun rise on the evil and on the good, and sends rain on the just and on the unjust.

MATTHEW 5:44–45

For this is commendable, if because of conscience toward God one endures grief, suffering wrongfully.

For what credit is it if, when you are beaten for your faults, you take it patiently? But when you do good and suffer, if you take it patiently, this is commendable before God. For to this you were called, because Christ also suffered for us, leaving us an example, that you should follow His steps:

"Who committed no sin,

Nor was deceit found in His mouth";

who, when He was reviled, did not revile in return; when He suffered, He did not threaten, but committed Himself to Him who judges righteously.

1 PETER 2:19–23

Do not say, "I will recompense evil";
Wait for the LORD, and He will save you.

PROVERBS 20:22

But love your enemies, do good, and lend, hoping for nothing in return; and your reward will be great, and you will be sons of the Most High. For He is kind to the unthankful and evil. . . . Judge not, and you shall not be judged. Condemn not, and you shall not be condemned. Forgive, and you will be forgiven.

LUKE 6:35, 37

Blessed are those who are persecuted for righteousness' sake, For theirs is the kingdom of heaven.

Blessed are you when they revile and persecute you, and say all kinds of evil against you falsely for My sake. Rejoice and be exceedingly glad, for great is your reward in heaven, for so they persecuted the prophets who were before you.

MATTHEW 5:11–12

Let all bitterness, wrath, anger, clamor, and evil speaking be put away from you, with all malice. And be kind to one another, tenderhearted, forgiving one another, even as God in Christ forgave you.

EPHESIANS 4:31–32

If you are reproached for the name of Christ, blessed are you, for the Spirit of glory and of God rests upon you. On their part He is blasphemed, but on your part He is glorified.

1 PETER 4:14

IN FELLOWSHIP

A new commandment I give to you, that you love one another; as I have loved you, that you also love one another. By this all will know that you are My disciples, if you have love for one another.

JOHN 13:34–35

Let the word of Christ dwell in you richly in all wisdom, teaching and admonishing one another in psalms and hymns and spiritual songs, singing with grace in your hearts to the Lord.

COLOSSIANS 3:16

And they continued steadfastly in the apostles' doctrine and fellowship, in the breaking of bread, and in prayers. . . . So continuing daily with one accord in the temple, and breaking bread from house to house, they ate their food with gladness and simplicity of heart, praising God and having favor with all the people. And the Lord added to the church daily those who were being saved.

ACTS 2:42, 46–47

Then those who feared the LORD spoke to one
    another,
And the LORD listened and heard them;
So a book of remembrance was written before Him
For those who fear the LORD
And who meditate on His name.

MALACHI 3:16

That their hearts may be encouraged, being knit together in love, and attaining to all riches of the full assurance of understanding, to the knowledge of the mystery of God, both of the Father and of Christ.

COLOSSIANS 2:2

And walk in love, as Christ also has loved us and given Himself for us, an offering and a sacrifice to God for a sweet-smelling aroma.

EPHESIANS 5:2

We took sweet counsel together,
And walked to the house of God in the throng.

PSALM 55:14

As iron sharpens iron,
So a man sharpens the countenance of his friend.

PROVERBS 27:17

God is faithful, by whom you were called into the fellowship of His Son, Jesus Christ our Lord.

1 CORINTHIANS 1:9

Two are better than one,
Because they have a good reward for their labor.
For if they fall, one will lift up his companion.
But woe to him who is alone when he falls,
For he has no one to help him up.

ECCLESIASTES 4:9–10

Let each of us please his neighbor for his good, leading to edification.

ROMANS 15:2

I have shown you in every way, by laboring like this, that you must support the weak. And remember the words of the Lord Jesus, that He said, "It is more blessed to give than to receive."

ACTS 20:35

A man who has friends must himself be friendly,
But there is a friend who sticks closer than a
  brother.

PROVERBS 18:24

IN HOLINESS

Blessed are the pure in heart,
  For they shall see God.

MATTHEW 5:8

To the pure all things are pure, but to those who are defiled and unbelieving nothing is pure; but even their mind and conscience are defiled.

TITUS 1:15

Who may ascend into the hill of the LORD?
Or who may stand in His holy place?
He who has clean hands and a pure heart,
Who has not lifted up his soul to an idol,
Nor sworn deceitfully.

PSALM 24:3–4

Who gave Himself for us, that He might redeem us from every lawless deed and purify for Himself His own special people, zealous for good works.

TITUS 2:14

To grant us that we,
Being delivered from the hand of our enemies,
Might serve Him without fear,
In holiness and righteousness before Him all the
    days of our life.

LUKE 1:74–75

And you, who once were alienated and enemies in your mind by wicked works, yet now He has reconciled in the body of His flesh through death, to present you holy, and blameless, and above reproach in His sight.

COLOSSIANS 1:21–22

And for their sakes I sanctify Myself, that they also may be sanctified by the truth.

JOHN 17:19

Now may the God of peace Himself sanctify you completely; and may your whole spirit, soul, and body be preserved blameless at the coming of our Lord Jesus Christ.

1 THESSALONIANS 5:23

And if Christ is in you, the body is dead because of sin, but the Spirit is life because of righteousness.

ROMANS 8:10

IN VICTORY OVER SIN

Then the Lord knows how to deliver the godly out of temptations and to reserve the unjust under punishment for the day of judgment.

2 PETER 2:9

For sin shall not have dominion over you, for you are not under law but under grace.

ROMANS 6:14

Therefore let him who thinks he stands take heed lest he fall. No temptation has overtaken you except such as is common to man; but God is faithful, who will not allow you to be tempted beyond what you are able, but with the temptation will also make the way of escape, that you may be able to bear it.

1 CORINTHIANS 10:12–13

For in that He Himself has suffered, being tempted, He is able to aid those who are tempted.

HEBREWS 2:18

Be sober, be vigilant; because your adversary the devil walks about like a roaring lion, seeking whom he may devour. Resist him, steadfast in the faith, knowing that the same sufferings are experienced by your brotherhood in the world.

1 PETER 5:8–9

Above all, taking the shield of faith with which you will be able to quench all the fiery darts of the wicked one.

EPHESIANS 6:16

You are of God, little children, and have overcome them, because He who is in you is greater than he who is in the world.

1 JOHN 4:4

Your word I have hidden in my heart,
That I might not sin against You.

PSALM 119:11

He who covers his sins will not prosper,
But whoever confesses and forsakes them will have
    mercy.

PROVERBS 28:13

Blessed is the man who endures temptation; for when he has been approved, he will receive the crown of life which the Lord has promised to those who love Him. Let no one say when he is tempted, "I am tempted by God"; for God cannot be tempted by evil, nor does He Himself tempt anyone. But each one is tempted when he is drawn away by his own desires and enticed.

JAMES 1:12–14

If we confess our sins, He is faithful and just to forgive us our sins and to cleanse us from all unrighteousness.

1 JOHN 1:9

Therefore submit to God. Resist the devil and he will flee from you.

JAMES 4:7

In this you greatly rejoice, though now for a little while, if need be, you have been grieved by various trials, that the genuineness of your faith, being much more precious than gold that perishes, though it is tested by fire, may be found to praise, honor, and glory at the revelation of Jesus Christ.

1 PETER 1:6–7

O wretched man that I am! Who will deliver me from this body of death? I thank God—through Jesus Christ our Lord! So then, with the mind I myself serve the law of God, but with the flesh the law of sin.

ROMANS 7:24–25

I say then: Walk in the Spirit, and you shall not
fulfill the lust of the flesh.

GALATIANS 5:16

Yet in all these things we are more than conquerors
through Him who loved us.

ROMANS 8:37

It is good that you grasp this,
And also not remove your hand from the other;
For he who fears God will escape them all.

ECCLESIASTES 7:18

For the law of the Spirit of life in Christ Jesus has
made me free from the law of sin and death. For
what the law could not do in that it was weak
through the flesh, God did by sending His own
Son in the likeness of sinful flesh, on account of
sin: He condemned sin in the flesh, that the
righteous requirement of the law might be fulfilled
in us who do not walk according to the flesh but
according to the Spirit.

ROMANS 8:2–4

IN FINDING HIS WILL

I will instruct you and teach you in the way you
   should go;
I will guide you with My eye.

PSALM 32:8

And we know that the Son of God has come and has given us an understanding, that we may know Him who is true; and we are in Him who is true, in His Son Jesus Christ. This is the true God and eternal life.

1 JOHN 5:20

If anyone wills to do His will, he shall know concerning the doctrine, whether it is from God or whether I speak on My own authority.

JOHN 7:17

Trust in the LORD with all your heart,
And lean not on your own understanding;
In all your ways acknowledge Him,
And He shall direct your paths.

PROVERBS 3:5–6

For I will give you a mouth and wisdom which all your adversaries will not be able to contradict or resist.

LUKE 21:15

However, when He, the Spirit of truth, has come, He will guide you into all truth; for He will not speak on His own authority, but whatever He hears He will speak; and He will tell you things to come.

JOHN 16:13

Evil men do not understand justice,
But those who seek the LORD understand all.

PROVERBS 28:5

Turn at my rebuke;
Surely I will pour out my spirit on you;
I will make my words known to you.

PROVERBS 1:23

The entrance of Your words gives light;
It gives understanding to the simple.

PSALM 119:130

Commit your works to the LORD,
And your thoughts will be established.

PROVERBS 16:3

Let us know,
Let us pursue the knowledge of the LORD.
His going forth is established as the morning;
He will come to us like the rain,
Like the latter and former rain to the earth.

HOSEA 6:3

For God gives wisdom and knowledge and joy to a
man who is good in His sight; but to the sinner He
gives the work of gathering and collecting, that he
may give to him who is good before God. This also
is vanity and grasping for the wind.

ECCLESIASTES 2:26

My soul, wait silently for God alone,
For my expectation is from Him.

PSALM 62:5

With Him are wisdom and strength,
He has counsel and understanding.

JOB 12:13

The LORD will perfect that which concerns me;
Your mercy, O LORD, endures forever;
Do not forsake the works of Your hands.

PSALM 138:8

Cast your burden on the LORD,
And He shall sustain you;
He shall never permit the righteous to be moved.

PSALM 55:22

For it is the God who commanded light to shine
out of darkness, who has shone in our hearts to
give the light of the knowledge of the glory of God
in the face of Jesus Christ.

2 CORINTHIANS 4:6

At that time Jesus answered and said, "I thank You,
Father, Lord of heaven and earth, that You have
hidden these things from the wise and prudent and
have revealed them to babes."

MATTHEW 11:25

But the natural man does not receive the things of the Spirit of God, for they are foolishness to him; nor can he know them, because they are spiritually discerned. But he who is spiritual judges all things, yet he himself is rightly judged by no one.

1 CORINTHIANS 2:14–15

IN SECURITY

You are of God, little children, and have overcome them, because He who is in you is greater than he who is in the world.

1 JOHN 4:4

My Father, who has given them to Me, is greater than all; and no one is able to snatch them out of My Father's hand.

JOHN 10:29

Now to Him who is able to keep you from
   stumbling,
And to present you faultless
Before the presence of His glory with exceeding joy,
To God our Savior,
Who alone is wise,
Be glory and majesty,
Dominion and power,
Both now and forever.
Amen.

JUDE 24–25

Why are you cast down, O my soul?
And why are you disquieted within me?
Hope in God, for I shall yet praise Him
For the help of His countenance.

PSALM 42:5

And it will be said in that day:
"Behold, this is our God;
We have waited for Him, and He will save us.
This is the LORD;
We have waited for Him;
We will be glad and rejoice in His salvation."

ISAIAH 25:9

And who is he who will harm you if you become
followers of what is good?

1 PETER 3:13

Lift up your eyes on high,
And see who has created these things,
Who brings out their host by number;
He calls them all by name,
By the greatness of His might
And the strength of His power;
Not one is missing.

ISAIAH 40:26

Being confident of this very thing, that He who has begun a good work in you will complete it until the day of Jesus Christ.

PHILIPPIANS 1:6

Therefore do not cast away your confidence, which has great reward. For you have need of endurance, so that after you have done the will of God, you may receive the promise.

HEBREWS 10:35–36

I can do all things through Christ who strengthens me.

PHILIPPIANS 4:13

So we may boldly say:
"The LORD is my helper;
I will not fear.
What can man do to me?"

HEBREWS 13:6

Now this is the confidence that we have in Him, that if we ask anything according to His will, He hears us. And if we know that He hears us, whatever we ask, we know that we have the petitions that we have asked of Him.

1 JOHN 5:14–15

We know that whoever is born of God does not sin; but he who has been born of God keeps himself, and the wicked one does not touch him.

1 JOHN 5:18

If I say, "My foot slips,"
Your mercy, O LORD, will hold me up.

PSALM 94:18

Therefore, brethren, be even more diligent to make your call and election sure, for if you do these things you will never stumble.

2 PETER 1:10

IN ANSWERED PRAYER

And whatever you ask in My name, that I will do, that the Father may be glorified in the Son. If you ask anything in My name, I will do it.

JOHN 14:13–14

And whatever we ask we receive from Him, because we keep His commandments and do those things that are pleasing in His sight.

1 JOHN 3:22

And whatever things you ask in prayer, believing, you will receive.

MATTHEW 21:22

If you abide in Me, and My words abide in you,
you will ask what you desire, and it shall be done
for you.

JOHN 15:7

And the prayer of faith will save the sick, and the
Lord will raise him up. And if he has committed
sins, he will be forgiven. Confess your trespasses to
one another, and pray for one another, that you
may be healed. The effective, fervent prayer of a
righteous man avails much.

JAMES 5:15–16

But know that the LORD has set apart for Himself
    him who is godly;
The LORD will hear when I call to Him.

PSALM 4:3

The eyes of the LORD are on the righteous,
And His ears are open to their cry. . . .
The righteous cry out, and the LORD hears,
And delivers them out of all their troubles.

PSALM 34:15, 17

The LORD is far from the wicked,
But He hears the prayer of the righteous.

PROVERBS 15:29

He shall call upon Me, and I will answer him;
I will be with him in trouble;
I will deliver him and honor him.

PSALM 91:15

It shall come to pass
That before they call, I will answer;
And while they are still speaking, I will hear.

ISAIAH 65:24

I will call upon the LORD, who is worthy to be
    praised;
So shall I be saved from my enemies.

PSALM 18:3

Call to Me, and I will answer you, and show you
great and mighty things, which you do not know.

JEREMIAH 33:3

IN PRAISE

But you are a chosen generation, a royal priesthood,
a holy nation, His own special people, that you
may proclaim the praises of Him who called you
out of darkness into His marvelous light.

1 PETER 2:9

Praise the LORD, all you Gentiles!
Laud Him, all you peoples!
For His merciful kindness is great toward us,

And the truth of the LORD endures forever.
Praise the LORD!

PSALM 117:1–2

But thanks be to God, who gives us the victory
through our Lord Jesus Christ.

1 CORINTHIANS 15:57

Oh, that men would give thanks to the LORD for
His goodness,
And for His wonderful works to the children of
men!

PSALM 107:8

This people I have formed for Myself;
They shall declare My praise.

ISAIAH 43:21

Praise the LORD!
For it is good to sing praises to our God;
For it is pleasant, and praise is beautiful.

PSALM 147:1

And in that day you will say:
"O LORD, I will praise You;
Though You were angry with me,
Your anger is turned away, and You comfort me."

ISAIAH 12:1

Praise the LORD!
Praise God in His sanctuary;
Praise Him in His mighty firmament!
Praise Him for His mighty acts;
Praise Him according to His excellent greatness!

PSALM 150:1–2

But I will sacrifice to You
With the voice of thanksgiving;
I will pay what I have vowed.
Salvation is of the LORD.

JONAH 2:9

Sing to God, you kingdoms of the earth;
Oh, sing praises to the Lord, Selah

PSALM 68:32

O LORD, You are my God.
I will exalt You,
I will praise Your name,
For You have done wonderful things;
Your counsels of old are faithfulness and truth.

ISAIAH 25:1

IN DEDICATION

For God is not unjust to forget your work and
labor of love which you have shown toward His
name, in that you have ministered to the saints,
and do minister.

HEBREWS 6:10

Let your light so shine before men, that they may see your good works and glorify your Father in heaven.

MATTHEW 5:16

But let each one examine his own work, and then he will have rejoicing in himself alone, and not in another.

GALATIANS 6:4

My little children, let us not love in word or in tongue, but in deed and in truth.

1 JOHN 3:18

And whoever gives one of these little ones only a cup of cold water in the name of a disciple, assuredly, I say to you, he shall by no means lose his reward.

MATTHEW 10:42

And He said to them, "Go into all the world and preach the gospel to every creature."

MARK 16:15

You are the salt of the earth; but if the salt loses its flavor, how shall it be seasoned? It is then good for nothing but to be thrown out and trampled underfoot by men. You are the light of the world. A city that is set on a hill cannot be hidden.

MATTHEW 5:13–14

By this we know love, because He laid down His life for us. And we also ought to lay down our lives for the brethren. But whoever has this world's goods, and sees his brother in need, and shuts up his heart from him, how does the love of God abide in him?

1 JOHN 3:16–17

Pure and undefiled religion before God and the Father is this: to visit orphans and widows in their trouble, and to keep oneself unspotted from the world.

JAMES 1:27

Now then, we are ambassadors for Christ, as though God were pleading through us: we implore you on Christ's behalf, be reconciled to God.

2 CORINTHIANS 5:20

For we are His workmanship, created in Christ Jesus for good works, which God prepared beforehand that we should walk in them.

EPHESIANS 2:10

Now all things are of God, who has reconciled us to Himself through Jesus Christ, and has given us the ministry of reconciliation.

2 CORINTHIANS 5:18

Let my heart be blameless regarding Your statutes,
That I may not be ashamed.

PSALM 119:80

For the LORD is righteous,
He loves righteousness;
His countenance beholds the upright.

PSALM 11:7

IN STEWARDSHIP

But this I say: He who sows sparingly will also reap
sparingly, and he who sows bountifully will also
reap bountifully. So let each one give as he purposes
in his heart, not grudgingly or of necessity; for God
loves a cheerful giver. And God is able to make all
grace abound toward you, that you, always having
all sufficiency in all things, may have an abundance
for every good work.

2 CORINTHIANS 9:6–8

Honor the LORD with your possessions,
And with the firstfruits of all your increase;
So your barns will be filled with plenty,
And your vats will overflow with new wine.

PROVERBS 3:9–10

Command those who are rich in this present age
not to be haughty, nor to trust in uncertain riches
but in the living God, who gives us richly all things

to enjoy. Let them do good, that they be rich in good works, ready to give, willing to share, storing up for themselves a good foundation for the time to come, that they may lay hold on eternal life.

1 TIMOTHY 6:17–19

Give, and it will be given to you: good measure, pressed down, shaken together, and running over will be put into your bosom. For with the same measure that you use, it will be measured back to you.

LUKE 6:38

Now concerning the collection for the saints, as I have given orders to the churches of Galatia, so you must do also: On the first day of the week let each one of you lay something aside, storing up as he may prosper, that there be no collections when I come.

1 CORINTHIANS 16:1–2

And whatever you do, do it heartily, as to the Lord and not to men, knowing that from the Lord you will receive the reward of the inheritance; for you serve the Lord Christ.

COLOSSIANS 3:23–24

And everyone who has left houses or brothers or sisters or father or mother or wife or children or lands, for My name's sake, shall receive a hundredfold, and inherit eternal life.

MATTHEW 19:29

Therefore keep the words of this covenant, and do them, that you may prosper in all that you do.

DEUTERONOMY 29:9

IN BENEVOLENT WORK

For God is not unjust to forget your work and labor of love which you have shown toward His name, in that you have ministered to the saints, and do minister.

HEBREWS 6:10

But do not forget to do good and to share, for with such sacrifices God is well pleased.

HEBREWS 13:16

Then Jesus, looking at him, loved him, and said to him, "One thing you lack: Go your way, sell whatever you have and give to the poor, and you will have treasure in heaven; and come, take up the cross, and follow Me."

MARK 10:21

He who gives to the poor will not lack,
But he who hides his eyes will have many curses.

PROVERBS 28:27

He who despises his neighbor sins;
But he who has mercy on the poor, happy is he.

PROVERBS 14:21

And God is able to make all grace abound toward
you, that you, always having all sufficiency in all
things, may have an abundance for every good
work.

2 CORINTHIANS 9:8

He who has pity on the poor lends to the LORD,
And He will pay back what he has given.

PROVERBS 19:17

My little children, let us not love in word or in
tongue, but in deed and in truth. And by this we
know that we are of the truth, and shall assure our
hearts before Him.

1 JOHN 3:18–19

He has dispersed abroad,
He has given to the poor;
His righteousness endures forever;
His horn will be exalted with honor.

PSALM 112:9

Give, and it will be given to you: good measure,
pressed down, shaken together, and running over
will be put into your bosom. For with the same

measure that you use, it will be measured back to you.

LUKE 6:38

Blessed is he who considers the poor;
The LORD will deliver him in time of trouble.
The LORD will preserve him and keep him alive,
And he will be blessed on the earth;
You will not deliver him to the will of his enemies.
The LORD will strengthen him on his bed of
    illness;
You will sustain him on his sickbed.

PSALM 41:1–3

He who has a generous eye will be blessed,
For he gives of his bread to the poor.

PROVERBS 22:9

Sell what you have and give alms; provide
yourselves money bags which do not grow old, a
treasure in the heavens that does not fail, where no
thief approaches nor moth destroys.

LUKE 12:33

IN OBEDIENCE

He who has My commandments and keeps them, it is he who loves Me. And he who loves Me will be loved by My Father, and I will love him and manifest Myself to him.

JOHN 14:21

And whatever we ask we receive from Him, because we keep His commandments and do those things that are pleasing in His sight.

1 JOHN 3:22

Therefore keep the words of this covenant, and do them, that you may prosper in all that you do.

DEUTERONOMY 29:9

For whoever does the will of My Father in heaven is My brother and sister and mother.

MATTHEW 12:50

But he who looks into the perfect law of liberty and continues in it, and is not a forgetful hearer but a doer of the work, this one will be blessed in what he does.

JAMES 1:25

He who keeps the commandment keeps his soul, But he who is careless of his ways will die.

PROVERBS 19:16

Now therefore, if you will indeed obey My voice and keep My covenant, then you shall be a special treasure to Me above all people; for all the earth is Mine.

EXODUS 19:5

Blessed are the undefiled in the way,
Who walk in the law of the LORD!
Blessed are those who keep His testimonies,
Who seek Him with the whole heart!

PSALM 119:1–2

If you are willing and obedient,
You shall eat the good of the land.

ISAIAH 1:19

And the world is passing away, and the lust of it; but he who does the will of God abides forever.

1 JOHN 2:17

If you know these things, blessed are you if you do them.

JOHN 13:17

IN PRAYER

Likewise the Spirit also helps in our weaknesses. For we do not know what we should pray for as we ought, but the Spirit Himself makes intercession for us with groanings which cannot be uttered.

ROMANS 8:26

Call to Me, and I will answer you, and show you great and mighty things, which you do not know.

JEREMIAH 33:3

Then He spoke a parable to them, that men always ought to pray and not lose heart.

LUKE 18:1

And shall God not avenge His own elect who cry out day and night to Him, though He bears long with them?

LUKE 18:7

Again I say to you that if two of you agree on earth concerning anything that they ask, it will be done for them by My Father in heaven. For where two or three are gathered together in My name, I am there in the midst of them.

MATTHEW 18:19–20

But you, when you pray, go into your room, and when you have shut your door, pray to your Father who is in the secret place; and your Father who sees in secret will reward you openly.

MATTHEW 6:6

Therefore I say to you, whatever things you ask when you pray, believe that you receive them, and you will have them.

MARK 11:24

The LORD is near to all who call upon Him,
To all who call upon Him in truth.
He will fulfill the desire of those who fear Him;
He also will hear their cry and save them.

PSALM 145:18–19

Delight yourself also in the LORD,
And He shall give you the desires of your heart.

PSALM 37:4

The LORD is far from the wicked,
But He hears the prayer of the righteous.

PROVERBS 15:29

He shall pray to God, and He will delight in him,
He shall see His face with joy,
For He restores to man His righteousness.

JOB 33:26

For what great nation is there that has God so near
to it, as the LORD our God is to us, for whatever
reason we may call upon Him?

DEUTERONOMY 4:7

For You, Lord, are good, and ready to forgive,
And abundant in mercy to all those who call upon
You.

PSALM 86:5

Draw near to God and He will draw near to you. Cleanse your hands, you sinners; and purify your hearts, you double-minded.

JAMES 4:8

But without faith it is impossible to please Him, for he who comes to God must believe that He is, and that He is a rewarder of those who diligently seek Him.

HEBREWS 11:6

Pray without ceasing, in everything give thanks; for this is the will of God in Christ Jesus for you.

1 THESSALONIANS 5:17–18

IN WITNESS

And Jesus came and spoke to them, saying, "All authority has been given to Me in heaven and on earth. Go therefore and make disciples of all the nations, baptizing them in the name of the Father and of the Son and of the Holy Spirit, teaching them to observe all things that I have commanded you; and lo, I am with you always, even to the end of the age." Amen.

MATTHEW 28:18–20

And He said to them, "Go into all the world and preach the gospel to every creature."

MARK 16:15

You therefore, my son, be strong in the grace that is in Christ Jesus. And the things that you have heard from me among many witnesses, commit these to faithful men who will be able to teach others also.

2 TIMOTHY 2:1–2

Then He said to them, "Thus it is written, and thus it was necessary for the Christ to suffer and to rise from the dead the third day, and that repentance and remission of sins should be preached in His name to all nations, beginning at Jerusalem. And you are witnesses of these things."

LUKE 24:46–48

Ask of Me, and I will give You
The nations for Your inheritance,
And the ends of the earth for Your possession.

PSALM 2:8

And I, if I am lifted up from the earth, will draw all peoples to Myself.

JOHN 12:32

And since we have the same spirit of faith, according to what is written, "I believed and therefore I spoke," we also believe and therefore speak.

2 CORINTHIANS 4:13

Indeed I have given him as a witness to the people,
A leader and commander for the people.
Surely you shall call a nation you do not know,
And nations who do not know you shall run to you,
Because of the LORD your God,
And the Holy One of Israel;
For He has glorified you.

ISAIAH 55:4–5

Now we exhort you, brethren, warn those who are
unruly, comfort the fainthearted, uphold the weak,
be patient with all.

1 THESSALONIANS 5:14

And this gospel of the kingdom will be preached in
all the world as a witness to all the nations, and
then the end will come.

MATTHEW 24:14

FROM BACKSLIDING

Behold, the LORD's hand is not shortened,
That it cannot save;
Nor His ear heavy,
That it cannot hear.
But your iniquities have separated you from your
    God;
And your sins have hidden His face from you,
So that He will not hear.

ISAIAH 59:1–2

For he who lacks these things is shortsighted, even to blindness, and has forgotten that he was cleansed from his old sins. Therefore, brethren, be even more diligent to make your call and election sure, for if you do these things you will never stumble.

2 PETER 1:9–10

For whatever is born of God overcomes the world. And this is the victory that has overcome the world—our faith. Who is he who overcomes the world, but he who believes that Jesus is the Son of God?

1 JOHN 5:4–5

Therefore submit to God. Resist the devil and he will flee from you. Draw near to God and He will draw near to you. Cleanse your hands, you sinners; and purify your hearts, you double-minded. Lament and mourn and weep! Let your laughter be turned to mourning and your joy to gloom. Humble yourselves in the sight of the Lord, and He will lift you up.

JAMES 4:7–10

Then the Lord knows how to deliver the godly out of temptations and to reserve the unjust under punishment for the day of judgment.

2 PETER 2:9

I say then: Walk in the Spirit, and you shall not fulfill the lust of the flesh.

GALATIANS 5:16

Do not boast about tomorrow,
For you do not know what a day may bring forth.

PROVERBS 27:1

Adulterers and adulteresses! Do you not know that friendship with the world is enmity with God? Whoever therefore wants to be a friend of the world makes himself an enemy of God. Or do you think that the Scripture says in vain, "The Spirit who dwells in us yearns jealously"? But He gives more grace. Therefore He says: "God resists the proud, But gives grace to the humble."

JAMES 4:4–6

O wretched man that I am! Who will deliver me from this body of death? I thank God—through Jesus Christ our Lord! So then, with the mind I myself serve the law of God, but with the flesh the law of sin.

ROMANS 7:24–25

He who covers his sins will not prosper,
But whoever confesses and forsakes them will have
    mercy.

PROVERBS 28:13

No temptation has overtaken you except such as is common to man; but God is faithful, who will not allow you to be tempted beyond what you are able, but with the temptation will also make the way of escape, that you may be able to bear it.

1 CORINTHIANS 10:13

Therefore, brethren, be even more diligent to make your call and election sure, for if you do these things you will never stumble.

2 PETER 1:10

The backslider in heart will be filled with his own
    ways,
But a good man will be satisfied from above.

PROVERBS 14:14

I will heal their backsliding,
I will love them freely,
For My anger has turned away from him.

HOSEA 14:4

~HE'LL~
LEAD YOU HOME

PROMISES FOR
YOUR PERSONAL NEEDS

L et me take you back to a day in 1994 that changed my life. I woke up restless at a quarter of six in the morning, thinking about what was going on in my life, and I wasn't happy about much of it. I felt that I'd failed at everything. I hadn't been a good friend, a good husband, a good father.

These feelings had been building up inside for a long time, and I didn't know what to do with the worthlessness that was eating away at me. I drove to the studio feeling really empty. Sometimes I go there to write but not this time. I wanted to be alone where I could cry out, "Help!

Help! I just can't do it. I'm out of steam. I don't have anything else to give."

It was an extremely emotional time of confession and pouring my heart out to God. Then I heard this voice saying, You're not supposed to do it. I'm going to lead you home. I know you're lost. I know you're alone. I'm going to finish the work. I'm going to take care of it.

Although I didn't intend to write, I sat down at the piano and wrote the music for "I'll Lead You Home." Wayne Kirkpatrick added most of the lyrics later to the only words that I had at the time: "Hear Me calling, hear Me calling. . . . Just leave it to Me, I'll lead you home." Judging from the letters people have written, the comfort that I received from that message has been multiplied in the lives of others who have heard this song.

We all have bad days like that, which cause us to question the purpose of our existence. Through the years, I've recorded a lot of songs addressing the hurts and scars that we carry with us. In fact, each song on The Big Picture album was a response to the mail I receive.

HARD TIMES

I don't know what burdens you carry or what thoughts haunt you when you try to sleep at night. This, however,

I do know. God is there in the pain. I can't explain why horrible things sometimes happen to good people, why young people die just when they seem to have their lives before them, why God doesn't miraculously heal diseases or rescue children from abusive situations.

Surely, Joseph thought the same thing when his brothers sold him into slavery, his employer's wife lied about his conduct, and he spent years in the king's prison. When he finally confronted his brothers about the misery they caused him, he said, "You meant evil against me; but God meant it for good" (Gen. 50:20).

You may not be familiar with a man from the Old Testament named Mephibosheth, but his story speaks clearly of God's provision (2 Sam. 9). Back in those days, it was standard practice for a ruling king to wipe out his rivals as well as their children, their servants, and sometimes even their animals. When David became king, most of Saul's household had been devastated. Yet David wanted to show kindness to the family because Saul's son, Jonathan, had been one of his dearest friends.

Mephibosheth, Jonathan's son, was found and brought into David's presence. Mephibosheth had every reason to believe that his life would be ended, but instead, the king decreed that the man and his family would dine at his royal banquet table as long as David reigned.

The Scripture goes to the trouble of telling us that Mephibosheth was lame in both feet. Running away wasn't even a viable option. Just when he might have expected the worst, he was given a position of honor.

God will provide—He will lead us home—but He doesn't necessarily give instant relief from our sufferings or release from our situations.

HIS TIMING—NOT OURS

The Israelites wandered around in the wilderness for forty years before God allowed them to move forward into the land He promised them. Abraham and Sarah didn't have their long-awaited son, Isaac, until Abraham was one hundred years old and Sarah was ninety. Simeon had anticipated Christ's arrival long before he encountered Mary and Joseph bringing their baby boy Jesus into the temple to undergo the rites of purification.

Still, God knows our needs even before we ask Him. In the Sermon on the Mount, Christ advised, "Ask, and it will be given to you; seek, and you will find; knock, and it will be opened to you. For everyone who asks receives, and he who seeks finds, and to him who knocks it will be opened" (Matt. 7:7–8).

A Sunday school teacher once said that the Greek words in this verse communicate the idea of persistent knocking. That requires something that I could always use more of—patience. Waiting is hard for me.

As a kid, I used to think that Christmas would never come. I loved everything about it—the food, the family gatherings, the presents, and especially the music. As an adult, I'm no different. I'm known for breaking out the Christmas albums really early and sneaking in a few "listens" throughout the year as well. With five kids, Christmas morning in our house is total chaos—and I love it. It's a blast watching my kids tear into their presents, model their new clothes, and play with their new toys.

In a way, the anticipation of Christmas is easy. Minute by minute, hour by hour, day by day, I know that December 25 is getting closer until it eventually arrives on schedule.

We can't be so sure about the timing in many areas of our lives, however. How long will it take to find a career that is genuinely rewarding? Will you find a mate today, two years from now, or never? It's impossible to lay down a timetable to things beyond our control.

To be hopeful is to be vulnerable to disappointment. Yet, without it, we become like Eeyore the donkey in the Winnie-the-Pooh stories, always expecting the worst in a situation.

God's best advice is to trust Him to provide for all of our needs (although not necessarily all our wants).

Cast your burden on the LORD,
And He shall sustain you;
He shall never permit the righteous to be moved.
(Ps. 55:22)

Just leave it to Him. He'll lead you home.

PROMISES FOR YOUR PERSONAL NEEDS

FOR TIMES OF LONELINESS

I will not leave you orphans; I will come to you.

JOHN 14:18

Let not your heart be troubled; you believe in God, believe also in Me.

JOHN 14:1

For I am persuaded that neither death nor life, nor angels nor principalities nor powers, nor things present nor things to come, nor height nor depth, nor any other created thing, shall be able to separate us from the love of God which is in Christ Jesus our Lord.

ROMANS 8:38–39

Casting all your care upon Him, for He cares for you.

1 PETER 5:7

The LORD also will be a refuge for the oppressed,
A refuge in times of trouble.
And those who know Your name will put their trust in You;
For You, LORD, have not forsaken those who seek You.

PSALM 9:9–10

Fear not, for I am with you;
Be not dismayed, for I am your God.
I will strengthen you,
Yes, I will help you,
I will uphold you with My righteous right hand.

ISAIAH 41:10

Who shall separate us from the love of Christ? Shall tribulation, or distress, or persecution, or famine, or nakedness, or peril, or sword? As it is written: "For Your sake we are killed all day long; we are accounted as sheep for the slaughter." Yet in

all these things we are more than conquerors
through Him who loved us.

ROMANS 8:35–37

Be strong and of good courage, do not fear nor be
afraid of them; for the LORD your God, He is the
One who goes with you. He will not leave you nor
forsake you.

DEUTERONOMY 31:6

In all their affliction He was afflicted,
And the Angel of His Presence saved them;
In His love and in His pity He redeemed them;
And He bore them and carried them
All the days of old.

ISAIAH 63:9

For the people shall dwell in Zion at Jerusalem;
You shall weep no more.
He will be very gracious to you at the sound of
    your cry;
When He hears it, He will answer you.

ISAIAH 30:19

Unto the upright there arises light in the darkness;
He is gracious, and full of compassion, and
    righteous.

PSALM 112:4

Therefore you now have sorrow; but I will see you again and your heart will rejoice, and your joy no one will take from you.

JOHN 16:22

Cast your burden on the LORD,
And He shall sustain you;
He shall never permit the righteous to be moved.

PSALM 55:22

FOR TIMES OF FEAR

Peace I leave with you, My peace I give to you; not as the world gives do I give to you. Let not your heart be troubled, neither let it be afraid.

JOHN 14:27

No evil shall befall you,
Nor shall any plague come near your dwelling;
For He shall give His angels charge over you,
To keep you in all your ways.

PSALM 91:10–11

For God has not given us a spirit of fear, but of power and of love and of a sound mind.

2 TIMOTHY 1:7

There is no fear in love; but perfect love casts out fear, because fear involves torment. But he who fears has not been made perfect in love.

1 JOHN 4:18

For you did not receive the spirit of bondage again to fear, but you received the Spirit of adoption by whom we cry out, "Abba, Father."

ROMANS 8:15

So we may boldly say:
"The LORD is my helper;
I will not fear.
What can man do to me?"

HEBREWS 13:6

He who dwells in the secret place of the Most High
Shall abide under the shadow of the Almighty.

PSALM 91:1

He shall cover you with His feathers,
And under His wings you shall take refuge;
His truth shall be your shield and buckler.
You shall not be afraid of the terror by night,
Nor of the arrow that flies by day,
Nor of the pestilence that walks in darkness,
Nor of the destruction that lays waste at noonday.
A thousand may fall at your side,
And ten thousand at your right hand;
But it shall not come near you.

PSALM 91:4–7

In righteousness you shall be established;
You shall be far from oppression, for you shall not
    fear;
And from terror, for it shall not come near you.

ISAIAH 54:14

God is our refuge and strength,
A very present help in trouble.

PSALM 46:1

The fear of man brings a snare,
But whoever trusts in the LORD shall be safe.

PROVERBS 29:25

Oh, how great is Your goodness,
Which You have laid up for those who fear You,
Which You have prepared for those who trust in You
In the presence of the sons of men!
You shall hide them in the secret place of Your
    presence
From the plots of man;
You shall keep them secretly in a pavilion
From the strife of tongues.

PSALM 31:19–20

You are my hiding place;
You shall preserve me from trouble;
You shall surround me with songs of deliverance.
    Selah

PSALM 32:7

The LORD is my light and my salvation;
Whom shall I fear?
The LORD is the strength of my life;
Of whom shall I be afraid?

PSALM 27:1

"No weapon formed against you shall prosper,
And every tongue which rises against you in
   judgment
You shall condemn.
This is the heritage of the servants of the LORD,
And their righteousness is from Me,"
Says the LORD.

ISAIAH 54:17

Do not be afraid of sudden terror,
Nor of trouble from the wicked when it comes;
For the LORD will be your confidence,
And will keep your foot from being caught.

PROVERBS 3:25–26

FOR TIMES OF ANGER

"Be angry, and do not sin": do not let the sun go
down on your wrath.

EPHESIANS 4:26

He who is slow to wrath has great understanding,
But he who is impulsive exalts folly.

PROVERBS 14:29

But now you yourselves are to put off all these:
anger, wrath, malice, blasphemy, filthy language
out of your mouth.

COLOSSIANS 3:8

A soft answer turns away wrath,
But a harsh word stirs up anger.

PROVERBS 15:1

A wrathful man stirs up strife,
But he who is slow to anger allays contention.

PROVERBS 15:18

For if you forgive men their trespasses, your
heavenly Father will also forgive you.

MATTHEW 6:14

He who is slow to anger is better than the mighty,
And he who rules his spirit than he who takes a
city.

PROVERBS 16:32

For we know Him who said, "Vengeance is Mine, I
will repay," says the Lord. And again, "The LORD
will judge His people."

HEBREWS 10:30

A fool's wrath is known at once,
But a prudent man covers shame.

PROVERBS 12:16

Cease from anger, and forsake wrath;
Do not fret—it only causes harm.

PSALM 37:8

A wise man fears and departs from evil,
But a fool rages and is self-confident.
A quick-tempered man acts foolishly,
And a man of wicked intentions is hated.

PROVERBS 14:16–17

An angry man stirs up strife,
And a furious man abounds in transgression.

PROVERBS 29:22

Do not hasten in your spirit to be angry,
For anger rests in the bosom of fools.

ECCLESIASTES 7:9

The discretion of a man makes him slow to anger,
And his glory is to overlook a transgression.

PROVERBS 19:11

A haughty look, a proud heart,
And the plowing of the wicked are sin.

PROVERBS 21:4

Scoffers set a city aflame,
But wise men turn away wrath.

PROVERBS 29:8

FOR TIMES OF FRUSTRATION

You will keep him in perfect peace,
Whose mind is stayed on You,
Because he trusts in You.

ISAIAH 26:3

Being confident of this very thing, that He who has
begun a good work in you will complete it until the
day of Jesus Christ.

PHILIPPIANS 1:6

Commit your way to the LORD,
Trust also in Him,
And He shall bring it to pass.

PSALM 37:5

For God is not the author of confusion but of
peace, as in all the churches of the saints.

1 CORINTHIANS 14:33

For where envy and self-seeking exist, confusion
and every evil thing are there. But the wisdom that
is from above is first pure, then peaceable, gentle,
willing to yield, full of mercy and good fruits,
without partiality and without hypocrisy. Now the
fruit of righteousness is sown in peace by those
who make peace.

JAMES 3:16–18

Trust in the LORD with all your heart,
And lean not on your own understanding;
In all your ways acknowledge Him,
And He shall direct your paths.

PROVERBS 3:5

If any of you lacks wisdom, let him ask of God,
who gives to all liberally and without reproach, and
it will be given to him.

JAMES 1:5

Be anxious for nothing, but in everything by prayer
and supplication, with thanksgiving, let your
requests be made known to God; and the peace of
God, which surpasses all understanding, will guard
your hearts and minds through Christ Jesus.

PHILIPPIANS 4:6–7

Rest in the LORD, and wait patiently for Him;
Do not fret because of him who prospers in his
    way,
Because of the man who brings wicked schemes to
    pass.

PSALM 37:7

Your ears shall hear a word behind you, saying,
"This is the way, walk in it,"
Whenever you turn to the right hand
Or whenever you turn to the left.

ISAIAH 30:21

The steps of a good man are ordered by the
   LORD,
And He delights in his way.

PSALM 37:23

Now this is the confidence that we have in Him,
that if we ask anything according to His will, He
hears us. And if we know that He hears us,
whatever we ask, we know that we have the
petitions that we have asked of Him.

1 JOHN 5:14–15

The LORD will perfect that which concerns me;
Your mercy, O LORD, endures forever;
Do not forsake the works of Your hands.

PSALM 138:8

He who did not spare His own Son, but delivered
Him up for us all, how shall He not with Him also
freely give us all things?

ROMANS 8:32

FOR TIMES OF GUILT

Most assuredly, I say to you, he who hears My word
and believes in Him who sent Me has everlasting
life, and shall not come into judgment, but has
passed from death into life.

JOHN 5:24

For if our heart condemns us, God is greater than our heart, and knows all things.

1 JOHN 3:20

If we confess our sins, He is faithful and just to forgive us our sins and to cleanse us from all unrighteousness.

1 JOHN 1:9

For God did not send His Son into the world to condemn the world, but that the world through Him might be saved. He who believes in Him is not condemned; but he who does not believe is condemned already, because he has not believed in the name of the only begotten Son of God.

JOHN 3:17–18

For I will be merciful to their unrighteousness, and their sins and their lawless deeds I will remember no more.

HEBREWS 8:12

I will cleanse them from all their iniquity by which they have sinned against Me, and I will pardon all their iniquities by which they have sinned and by which they have transgressed against Me.

JEREMIAH 33:8

"No more shall every man teach his neighbor, and every man his brother, saying, 'Know the LORD,' for they all shall know Me, from the least of them to the greatest of them, says the LORD. For I will forgive their iniquity, and their sin I will remember no more."

JEREMIAH 31:34

Let us draw near with a true heart in full assurance of faith, having our hearts sprinkled from an evil conscience and our bodies washed with pure water.

HEBREWS 10:22

Blessed is he whose transgression is forgiven,
Whose sin is covered.

PSALM 32:1

I acknowledged my sin to You,
And my iniquity I have not hidden.
I said, "I will confess my transgressions to the
    LORD,"
And You forgave the iniquity of my sin. Selah

PSALM 32:5

I, even I, am He who blots out your transgressions
    for My own sake;
And I will not remember your sins.

ISAIAH 43:25

"Therefore I say to you, her sins, which are many, are forgiven, for she loved much. But to whom little is forgiven, the same loves little." Then He said to her, "Your sins are forgiven."

LUKE 7:47–48

Then He said to the woman, "Your faith has saved you. Go in peace."

LUKE 7:50

Who is a God like You,
Pardoning iniquity
And passing over the transgression of the remnant
    of His heritage?
He does not retain His anger forever,
Because He delights in mercy.
He will again have compassion on us,
And will subdue our iniquities.
You will cast all our sins
Into the depths of the sea.

MICAH 7:18–19

For by one offering He has perfected forever those who are being sanctified. But the Holy Spirit also witnesses to us; for after He had said before, "This is the covenant that I will make with them after those days, says the LORD: I will put My laws into their hearts, and in their minds I will write them," then He adds, "Their sins and their lawless deeds I will remember no more."

HEBREWS 10:14–17

I have blotted out, like a thick cloud, your
   transgressions,
And like a cloud, your sins.
Return to Me, for I have redeemed you.

ISAIAH 44:22

FOR TIMES OF REBELLION

Let this mind be in you which was also in Christ
Jesus, who, being in the form of God, did not
consider it robbery to be equal with God, but made
Himself of no reputation, taking the form of a
bondservant, and coming in the likeness of men.
And being found in appearance as a man, He
humbled Himself and became obedient to the
point of death, even the death of the cross.

PHILIPPIANS 2:5–8

Obey those who rule over you, and be submissive,
for they watch out for your souls, as those who
must give account. Let them do so with joy and not
with grief, for that would be unprofitable for you.

HEBREWS 13:17

Therefore submit yourselves to every ordinance of
man for the Lord's sake, whether to the king as
supreme, or to governors, as to those who are sent
by him for the punishment of evildoers and for the
praise of those who do good. For this is the will of

God, that by doing good you may put to silence
the ignorance of foolish men.

1 PETER 2:13–15

This I say, therefore, and testify in the Lord, that
you should no longer walk as the rest of the
Gentiles walk, in the futility of their mind, having
their understanding darkened, being alienated from
the life of God, because of the ignorance that is in
them, because of the blindness of their heart.

EPHESIANS 4:17–18

No grave trouble will overtake the righteous,
But the wicked shall be filled with evil.

PROVERBS 12:21

For you were once darkness, but now you are light
in the Lord. Walk as children of light.

EPHESIANS 5:8

For the weapons of our warfare are not carnal but
mighty in God for pulling down strongholds,
casting down arguments and every high thing that
exalts itself against the knowledge of God, bringing
every thought into captivity to the obedience of
Christ.

2 CORINTHIANS 10:4–5

Not forsaking the assembling of ourselves together, as is the manner of some, but exhorting one another, and so much the more as you see the Day approaching.

HEBREWS 10:25

Blessed are those who do His commandments, that they may have the right to the tree of life, and may enter through the gates into the city.

REVELATION 22:14

"Return, you backsliding children,
And I will heal your backslidings.
Indeed we do come to You,
For You are the LORD our God."

JEREMIAH 3:22

FOR TIMES OF SUFFERING

For as the sufferings of Christ abound in us, so our consolation also abounds through Christ.

2 CORINTHIANS 1:5

And our hope for you is steadfast, because we know that as you are partakers of the sufferings, so also you will partake of the consolation.

2 CORINTHIANS 1:7

These things I have spoken to you, that in Me you may have peace. In the world you will have tribulation; but be of good cheer, I have overcome the world.

JOHN 16:33

We are confident, yes, well pleased rather to be absent from the body and to be present with the Lord. Therefore we make it our aim, whether present or absent, to be well pleasing to Him. For we must all appear before the judgment seat of Christ, that each one may receive the things done in the body, according to what he has done, whether good or bad.

2 CORINTHIANS 5:8–10

Is anyone among you suffering? Let him pray. Is anyone cheerful? Let him sing psalms.

JAMES 5:13

For He has not despised nor abhorred the affliction
    of the afflicted;
Nor has He hidden His face from Him;
But when He cried to Him, He heard.

PSALM 22:24

Wait on the LORD;
Be of good courage,
And He shall strengthen your heart;
Wait, I say, on the LORD!

PSALM 27:14

Cast your burden on the LORD,
And He shall sustain you;
He shall never permit the righteous to be moved.

PSALM 55:22

For a righteous man may fall seven times
And rise again,
But the wicked shall fall by calamity.

PROVERBS 24:16

The LORD upholds all who fall,
And raises up all who are bowed down.

PSALM 145:14

For the Lord will not cast off forever.
Though He causes grief,
Yet He will show compassion
According to the multitude of His mercies.
For He does not afflict willingly,
Nor grieve the children of men.

LAMENTATIONS 3:31–33

No grave trouble will overtake the righteous,
But the wicked shall be filled with evil.

PROVERBS 12:21

For His anger is but for a moment,
His favor is for life;
Weeping may endure for a night,
But joy comes in the morning.

PSALM 30:5

Many are the afflictions of the righteous,
But the LORD delivers him out of them all.

PSALM 34:19

Why are you cast down, O my soul?
And why are you disquieted within me?
Hope in God;
For I shall yet praise Him,
The help of my countenance and my God.

PSALM 42:11

You, who have shown me great and severe troubles,
Shall revive me again,
And bring me up again from the depths of the
    earth.

PSALM 71:20

FOR TIMES OF DISCOURAGEMENT

And let us not grow weary while doing good, for in
due season we shall reap if we do not lose heart.

GALATIANS 6:9

I would have lost heart, unless I had believed
That I would see the goodness of the LORD
In the land of the living.
Wait on the LORD;
Be of good courage,
And He shall strengthen your heart;
Wait, I say, on the LORD!

PSALM 27:13–14

So the ransomed of the LORD shall return,
And come to Zion with singing,
With everlasting joy on their heads.
They shall obtain joy and gladness;
Sorrow and sighing shall flee away.

ISAIAH 51:11

We are hard pressed on every side, yet not crushed;
we are perplexed, but not in despair; persecuted,
but not forsaken; struck down, but not destroyed.

2 CORINTHIANS 4:8–9

Though I walk in the midst of trouble, You will
revive me;
You will stretch out Your hand
Against the wrath of my enemies,
And Your right hand will save me.

PSALM 138:7

Let not your heart be troubled; you believe in God,
believe also in Me.

JOHN 14:1

Peace I leave with you, My peace I give to you; not
as the world gives do I give to you. Let not your
heart be troubled, neither let it be afraid.

JOHN 14:27

Be of good courage,
And He shall strengthen your heart,
All you who hope in the LORD.

PSALM 31:24

As a father pities his children,
So the LORD pities those who fear Him.
For He knows our frame;
He remembers that we are dust.

PSALM 103:13–14

The eternal God is your refuge,
And underneath are the everlasting arms;
He will thrust out the enemy from before you,
And will say, "Destroy!"

DEUTERONOMY 33:27

Behold, God will not cast away the blameless,
Nor will He uphold the evildoers.

JOB 8:20

But know that the LORD has set apart for Himself
    him who is godly;
The LORD will hear when I call to Him.

PSALM 4:3

For You, O LORD, will bless the righteous;
With favor You will surround him as with a shield.

PSALM 5:12

For the LORD loves justice,
And does not forsake His saints;
They are preserved forever,
But the descendants of the wicked shall be cut off.

PSALM 37:28

Wait on the LORD,
And keep His way,
And He shall exalt you to inherit the land;
When the wicked are cut off, you shall see it.

PSALM 37:34

Let us know,
Let us pursue the knowledge of the LORD.
His going forth is established as the morning;
He will come to us like the rain,
Like the latter and former rain to the earth.

HOSEA 6:3

FOR TIMES OF DEPRESSION

Finally, brethren, whatever things are true, whatever
things are noble, whatever things are just, whatever
things are pure, whatever things are lovely, whatever
things are of good report, if there is any virtue and
if there is anything praiseworthy—meditate on
these things.

PHILIPPIANS 4:8

Therefore humble yourselves under the mighty hand of God, that He may exalt you in due time, casting all your care upon Him, for He cares for you.

1 PETER 5:6–7

Beloved, do not think it strange concerning the fiery trial which is to try you, as though some strange thing happened to you; but rejoice to the extent that you partake of Christ's sufferings, that when His glory is revealed, you may also be glad with exceeding joy.

1 PETER 4:12–13

Fear not, for I am with you;
Be not dismayed, for I am your God.
I will strengthen you,
Yes, I will help you,
I will uphold you with My righteous right hand.

ISAIAH 41:10

So the ransomed of the LORD shall return,
And come to Zion with singing,
With everlasting joy on their heads.
They shall obtain joy and gladness;
Sorrow and sighing shall flee away.

ISAIAH 51:11

He heals the brokenhearted
And binds up their wounds.

PSALM 147:3

But I fear, lest somehow, as the serpent deceived
Eve by his craftiness, so your minds may be
corrupted from the simplicity that is in Christ. For
if he who comes preaches another Jesus whom we
have not preached, or if you receive a different
spirit which you have not received, or a different
gospel which you have not accepted—you may well
put up with it!

2 CORINTHIANS 11:3–4

The eyes of the LORD are on the righteous,
And His ears are open to their cry.

PSALM 34:15

The righteous cry out, and the LORD hears,
And delivers them out of all their troubles.

PSALM 34:17

Can a woman forget her nursing child,
And not have compassion on the son of her womb?
Surely they may forget,
Yet I will not forget you.
See, I have inscribed you on the palms of My
      hands;
Your walls are continually before Me.

ISAIAH 49:15–16

Blessed is the man who trusts in the LORD,
And whose hope is the LORD.
For he shall be like a tree planted by the waters,
Which spreads out its roots by the river,
And will not fear when heat comes;
But its leaf will be green,
And will not be anxious in the year of drought,
Nor will cease from yielding fruit.

JEREMIAH 17:7–8

And God will wipe away every tear from their eyes;
there shall be no more death, nor sorrow, nor
crying. There shall be no more pain, for the former
things have passed away.

REVELATION 21:4

FOR TIMES OF TROUBLE

Let not your heart be troubled; you believe in God,
believe also in Me.

JOHN 14:1

Peace I leave with you, My peace I give to you; not
as the world gives do I give to you. Let not your
heart be troubled, neither let it be afraid.

JOHN 14:27

For this cause everyone who is godly shall pray to
You
In a time when You may be found;

Surely in a flood of great waters
They shall not come near him.
You are my hiding place;
You shall preserve me from trouble;
You shall surround me with songs of deliverance.
  Selah

PSALM 32:6–7

We are hard pressed on every side, yet not crushed;
we are perplexed, but not in despair; persecuted,
but not forsaken; struck down, but not destroyed.

2 CORINTHIANS 4:8–9

Blessed be the God and Father of our Lord Jesus
Christ, the Father of mercies and God of all
comfort, who comforts us in all our tribulation,
that we may be able to comfort those who are in
any trouble, with the comfort with which we
ourselves are comforted by God.

2 CORINTHIANS 1:3–4

The LORD also will be a refuge for the oppressed,
A refuge in times of trouble.

PSALM 9:9

Though he fall, he shall not be utterly cast down;
For the LORD upholds him with His hand.

PSALM 37:24

But the salvation of the righteous is from the
    LORD;
He is their strength in the time of trouble.

PSALM 37:39

The wicked is ensnared by the transgression of his
    lips,
But the righteous will come through trouble.

PROVERBS 12:13

No grave trouble will overtake the righteous,
But the wicked shall be filled with evil.

PROVERBS 12:21

Blessed is he who considers the poor;
The LORD will deliver him in time of trouble.

PSALM 41:1

Though I walk in the midst of trouble, You will
    revive me;
You will stretch out Your hand
Against the wrath of my enemies,
And Your right hand will save me.

PSALM 138:7

He shall deliver you in six troubles,
Yes, in seven no evil shall touch you.

JOB 5:19

Then they cried out to the LORD in their trouble,
And He saved them out of their distresses.

PSALM 107:19

The LORD is good,
A stronghold in the day of trouble;
And He knows those who trust in Him.

NAHUM 1:7

Therefore I say to you, do not worry about your
life, what you will eat or what you will drink; nor
about your body, what you will put on. Is not life
more than food and the body more than clothing?
Look at the birds of the air, for they neither sow
nor reap nor gather into barns; yet your heavenly
Father feeds them. Are you not of more value than
they? Which of you by worrying can add one cubit
to his stature? So why do you worry about
clothing? Consider the lilies of the field, how they
grow: they neither toil nor spin; and yet I say to
you that even Solomon in all his glory was not
arrayed like one of these. Now if God so clothes
the grass of the field, which today is, and tomorrow
is thrown into the oven, will He not much more
clothe you, O you of little faith? Therefore do not
worry, saying, "What shall we eat?" or "What shall
we drink?" or "What shall we wear?" For after all
these things the Gentiles seek. For your heavenly
Father knows that you need all these things. But
seek first the kingdom of God and His

righteousness, and all these things shall be added to you. Therefore do not worry about tomorrow, for tomorrow will worry about its own things. Sufficient for the day is its own trouble.

MATTHEW 6:25–34

FOR TIMES OF NEED

The LORD is my shepherd;
I shall not want.

PSALM 23:1

I will deliver you from all your uncleannesses. I will call for the grain and multiply it, and bring no famine upon you. And I will multiply the fruit of your trees and the increase of your fields, so that you need never again bear the reproach of famine among the nations.

EZEKIEL 36:29–30

For He satisfies the longing soul,
And fills the hungry soul with goodness.

PSALM 107:9

But He answered and said, "It is written, 'Man shall not live by bread alone, but by every word that proceeds from the mouth of God.'"

MATTHEW 4:4

They shall not be ashamed in the evil time,
And in the days of famine they shall be satisfied.

PSALM 37:19

For the needy shall not always be forgotten;
The expectation of the poor shall not perish
     forever.

PSALM 9:18

He raises the poor out of the dust,
And lifts the needy out of the ash heap.

PSALM 113:7

He shall regard the prayer of the destitute,
And shall not despise their prayer.

PSALM 102:17

Listen, my beloved brethren: Has God not chosen
the poor of this world to be rich in faith and heirs
of the kingdom which He promised to those who
love Him?

JAMES 2:5

But Abraham said, "Son, remember that in your
lifetime you received your good things, and likewise
Lazarus evil things; but now he is comforted and
you are tormented."

LUKE 16:25

Sing to the LORD! Praise the LORD!
For He has delivered the life of the poor
From the hand of evildoers.

JEREMIAH 20:13

FOR TIMES OF TEMPTATION

O wretched man that I am! Who will deliver me
from this body of death? I thank God—through
Jesus Christ our Lord! So then, with the mind I
myself serve the law of God, but with the flesh the
law of sin.

ROMANS 7:24–25

No temptation has overtaken you except such as is
common to man; but God is faithful, who will not
allow you to be tempted beyond what you are able,
but with the temptation will also make the way of
escape, that you may be able to bear it.

1 CORINTHIANS 10:13

I say then: Walk in the Spirit, and you shall not
fulfill the lust of the flesh.

GALATIANS 5:16

For in that He Himself has suffered, being
tempted, He is able to aid those who are tempted.

HEBREWS 2:18

Then the Lord knows how to deliver the godly out of temptations and to reserve the unjust under punishment for the day of judgment.

2 PETER 2:9

You are of God, little children, and have overcome them, because He who is in you is greater than he who is in the world.

1 JOHN 4:4

Knowing this, that our old man was crucified with Him, that the body of sin might be done away with, that we should no longer be slaves of sin.

ROMANS 6:6

For sin shall not have dominion over you, for you are not under law but under grace.

ROMANS 6:14

In this you greatly rejoice, though now for a little while, if need be, you have been grieved by various trials, that the genuineness of your faith, being much more precious than gold that perishes, though it is tested by fire, may be found to praise, honor, and glory at the revelation of Jesus Christ.

1 PETER 1:6–7

Yet in all these things we are more than conquerors through Him who loved us.

ROMANS 8:37

These things I have spoken to you, that in Me you may have peace. In the world you will have tribulation; but be of good cheer, I have overcome the world.

JOHN 16:33

Finally, my brethren, be strong in the Lord and in the power of His might. Put on the whole armor of God, that you may be able to stand against the wiles of the devil. . . . Above all, taking the shield of faith with which you will be able to quench all the fiery darts of the wicked one.

EPHESIANS 6:10–11, 16

Who gave Himself for our sins, that He might deliver us from this present evil age, according to the will of our God and Father.

GALATIANS 1:4

Therefore submit to God. Resist the devil and he will flee from you.

JAMES 4:7

Blessed is the man who endures temptation; for when he has been approved, he will receive the crown of life which the Lord has promised to those who love Him. Let no one say when he is tempted, "I am tempted by God"; for God cannot be tempted by evil, nor does He Himself tempt anyone. But each one is tempted when he is drawn away by his own desires and enticed.

JAMES 1:12–14

For whatever is born of God overcomes the world. And this is the victory that has overcome the world—our faith. Who is he who overcomes the world, but he who believes that Jesus is the Son of God?

1 JOHN 5:4–5

Be sober, be vigilant; because your adversary the devil walks about like a roaring lion, seeking whom he may devour. Resist him, steadfast in the faith, knowing that the same sufferings are experienced by your brotherhood in the world.

1 PETER 5:8–9

I do not pray that You should take them out of the world, but that You should keep them from the evil one.

JOHN 17:15

But God forbid that I should boast except in the cross of our Lord Jesus Christ, by whom the world has been crucified to me, and I to the world.

GALATIANS 6:14

And the God of peace will crush Satan under your feet shortly. The grace of our Lord Jesus Christ be with you. Amen.

ROMANS 16:20

FOR TIMES OF IMPATIENCE

That you do not become sluggish, but imitate those who through faith and patience inherit the promises.

HEBREWS 6:12

And not only that, but we also glory in tribulations, knowing that tribulation produces perseverance; and perseverance, character; and character, hope. Now hope does not disappoint, because the love of God has been poured out in our hearts by the Holy Spirit who was given to us.

ROMANS 5:3–5

Therefore we also, since we are surrounded by so great a cloud of witnesses, let us lay aside every weight, and the sin which so easily ensnares us, and let us run with endurance the race that is set before us.

HEBREWS 12:1

Knowing that the testing of your faith produces patience. But let patience have its perfect work, that you may be perfect and complete, lacking nothing.

JAMES 1:3–4

Therefore do not cast away your confidence, which has great reward. For you have need of endurance, so that after you have done the will of God, you may receive the promise: "For yet a little while, and He who is coming will come and will not tarry."

HEBREWS 10:35–37

Therefore be patient, brethren, until the coming of the Lord. See how the farmer waits for the precious fruit of the earth, waiting patiently for it until it receives the early and latter rain. You also be patient. Establish your hearts, for the coming of the Lord is at hand.

JAMES 5:7–8

I waited patiently for the LORD;
And He inclined to me,
And heard my cry.

PSALM 40:1

But the fruit of the Spirit is love, joy, peace, longsuffering, kindness, goodness, faithfulness.

GALATIANS 5:22

But the ones that fell on the good ground are those who, having heard the word with a noble and good heart, keep it and bear fruit with patience.

LUKE 8:15

It is good that one should hope and wait quietly
For the salvation of the LORD.

LAMENTATIONS 3:26

By your patience possess your souls.

LUKE 21:19

Eternal life to those who by patient continuance in doing good seek for glory, honor, and immortality.

ROMANS 2:7

But if we hope for what we do not see, we eagerly wait for it with perseverance.

ROMANS 8:25

And it will be said in that day:
"Behold, this is our God;
We have waited for Him, and He will save us.
This is the LORD;
We have waited for Him;
We will be glad and rejoice in His salvation."

ISAIAH 25:9

FOR TIMES OF SICKNESS

Is anyone among you sick? Let him call for the
elders of the church, and let them pray over him,
anointing him with oil in the name of the Lord.
And the prayer of faith will save the sick, and the
Lord will raise him up. And if he has committed
sins, he will be forgiven.

JAMES 5:14–15

If you diligently heed the voice of the LORD your
God and do what is right in His sight, give ear to
His commandments and keep all His statutes, I will
put none of the diseases on you which I have
brought on the Egyptians. For I am the LORD who
heals you.

EXODUS 15:26

Surely He shall deliver you from the snare of the
    fowler
And from the perilous pestilence. . . .
You shall not be afraid of the terror by night,
Nor of the arrow that flies by day,
Nor of the pestilence that walks in darkness,
Nor of the destruction that lays waste at
    noonday. . . .
No evil shall befall you,
Nor shall any plague come near your dwelling.

PSALM 91:3. 5–6, 10

So you shall serve the LORD your God, and He will bless your bread and your water. And I will take sickness away from the midst of you.

EXODUS 23:25

The LORD will strengthen him on his bed of
  illness;
You will sustain him on his sickbed.

PSALM 41:3

Behold, I will bring it health and healing; I will heal them and reveal to them the abundance of peace and truth.

JEREMIAH 33:6

Beloved, I pray that you may prosper in all things and be in health, just as your soul prospers.

3 JOHN 1:2

He sent His word and healed them,
And delivered them from their destructions.

PSALM 107:20

Then Jesus went about all the cities and villages, teaching in their synagogues, preaching the gospel of the kingdom, and healing every sickness and every disease among the people.

MATTHEW 9:35

O LORD my God, I cried out to You,
And You healed me.

PSALM 30:2

Heal me, O LORD, and I shall be healed;
Save me, and I shall be saved,
For You are my praise.

JEREMIAH 17:14

And the whole multitude sought to touch Him, for
power went out from Him and healed them all.

LUKE 6:19

Come, and let us return to the LORD;
For He has torn, but He will heal us;
He has stricken, but He will bind us up.

HOSEA 6:1

My son, give attention to my words;
Incline your ear to my sayings.
Do not let them depart from your eyes;
Keep them in the midst of your heart;
For they are life to those who find them,
And health to all their flesh.

PROVERBS 4:20–22

FOR TIMES OF SADNESS

Blessed are those who mourn,
For they shall be comforted.

MATTHEW 5:4

Now may our Lord Jesus Christ Himself, and our
God and Father, who has loved us and given us
everlasting consolation and good hope by grace,
comfort your hearts and establish you in every
good word and work.

2 THESSALONIANS 2:16

Most assuredly, I say to you that you will weep and
lament, but the world will rejoice; and you will be
sorrowful, but your sorrow will be turned into joy.
A woman, when she is in labor, has sorrow because
her hour has come; but as soon as she has given
birth to the child, she no longer remembers the
anguish, for joy that a human being has been born
into the world. Therefore you now have sorrow;
but I will see you again and your heart will rejoice,
and your joy no one will take from you.

JOHN 16:20–22

This is my comfort in my affliction,
For Your word has given me life.

PSALM 119:50

So the ransomed of the LORD shall return,
And come to Zion with singing,
With everlasting joy on their heads.
They shall obtain joy and gladness;
Sorrow and sighing shall flee away.

ISAIAH 51:11

For we do not have a High Priest who cannot sympathize with our weaknesses, but was in all points tempted as we are, yet without sin. Let us therefore come boldly to the throne of grace, that we may obtain mercy and find grace to help in time of need.

HEBREWS 4:15–16

Blessed be the God and Father of our Lord Jesus Christ, the Father of mercies and God of all comfort, who comforts us in all our tribulation, that we may be able to comfort those who are in any trouble, with the comfort with which we ourselves are comforted by God.

2 CORINTHIANS 1:3–4

And those who know Your name will put their trust
in You;
For You, LORD, have not forsaken those who seek
You.

PSALM 9:10

When my father and my mother forsake me,
Then the LORD will take care of me.

PSALM 27:10

Persecuted, but not forsaken; struck down, but not destroyed.

2 CORINTHIANS 4:9

I have been young, and now am old;
Yet I have not seen the righteous forsaken,
Nor his descendants begging bread.

PSALM 37:25

The poor and needy seek water, but there is none,
Their tongues fail for thirst.
I, the LORD, will hear them;
I, the God of Israel, will not forsake them.

ISAIAH 41:17

Because he has set his love upon Me, therefore I
    will deliver him;
I will set him on high, because he has known My
    name.
He shall call upon Me, and I will answer him;
I will be with him in trouble;
I will deliver him and honor him.

PSALM 91:14–15

But as it is written:
"Eye has not seen, nor ear heard,

Nor have entered into the heart of man
The things which God has prepared for those who
    love Him."

1 CORINTHIANS 2:9

FOR TIMES OF BEREAVEMENT

But I do not want you to be ignorant, brethren,
concerning those who have fallen asleep, lest you
sorrow as others who have no hope. For if we
believe that Jesus died and rose again, even so God
will bring with Him those who sleep in Jesus.

1 THESSALONIANS 4:13–14

Yea, though I walk through the valley of the
    shadow of death,
I will fear no evil;
For You are with me;
Your rod and Your staff, they comfort me.

PSALM 23:4

For we know that if our earthly house, this tent, is
destroyed, we have a building from God, a house
not made with hands, eternal in the heavens. For in
this we groan, earnestly desiring to be clothed with
our habitation which is from heaven, if indeed,
having been clothed, we shall not be found naked.
For we who are in this tent groan, being burdened,
not because we want to be unclothed, but further

clothed, that mortality may be swallowed up by life.

2 CORINTHIANS 5:1–4

And God will wipe away every tear from their eyes; there shall be no more death, nor sorrow, nor crying. There shall be no more pain, for the former things have passed away.

REVELATION 21:4

Now He who has prepared us for this very thing is God, who also has given us the Spirit as a guarantee. So we are always confident, knowing that while we are at home in the body we are absent from the Lord. For we walk by faith, not by sight. We are confident, yes, well pleased rather to be absent from the body and to be present with the Lord.

2 CORINTHIANS 5:5–7

"O Death, where is your sting? O Hades, where is your victory?" The sting of death is sin, and the strength of sin is the law. But thanks be to God, who gives us the victory through our Lord Jesus Christ.

1 CORINTHIANS 15:55–57

Blessed be the God and Father of our Lord Jesus Christ, the Father of mercies and God of all comfort, who comforts us in all our tribulation, that we may be able to comfort those who are in any trouble, with the comfort with which we ourselves are comforted by God.

2 CORINTHIANS 1:3–4

But as it is written:
"Eye has not seen, nor ear heard,
Nor have entered into the heart of man
The things which God has prepared for those who love Him."

1 CORINTHIANS 2:9

And you will be blessed, because they cannot repay you; for you shall be repaid at the resurrection of the just.

LUKE 14:14

He will redeem his soul from going down to the Pit,
And his life shall see the light.

JOB 33:28

Precious in the sight of the LORD
Is the death of His saints.

PSALM 116:15

Our God is the God of salvation;
And to GOD the Lord belong escapes from death.

PSALM 68:20

For since by man came death, by Man also came
the resurrection of the dead. For as in Adam all die,
even so in Christ all shall be made alive.

1 CORINTHIANS 15:21–22

Jesus said to her, "I am the resurrection and the life.
He who believes in Me, though he may die, he shall
live."

JOHN 11:25

Blessed are those who mourn,
For they shall be comforted.

MATTHEW 5:4

Sing, O heavens!
Be joyful, O earth!
And break out in singing, O mountains!
For the LORD has comforted His people,
And will have mercy on His afflicted.

ISAIAH 49:13

~ You ~
WEREN'T MADE
TO LIVE ALONE

PROMISES FOR
VARIOUS RELATIONSHIPS

O f all the trips I've made, only a few top the
three treks to Mount LeConte in the Great Smoky Mountains National Park with a group of men drawn together
by my pastor. To illustrate the importance of honesty in relationships, let me take you on one of those trips.

Anywhere from fifty to sixty men load up in cars and
drive about four hours to the tourist-filled town of Pigeon
Forge, just a few miles from the park. Conversations
along the way might be a hodgepodge of small talk about
family, work, home repairs, cars, sports—all the typical
guy stuff. We rendezvous at a budget-priced hotel and
check in, then head out for a big dinner at a local restau-

rant. As we pass biscuits and preserves, we swap stories and laugh.

Next come the go-cart races. We might range in age from twenty to sixty-five, but once we get behind the wheel, every one of us drives like a kid. I've seen mild-mannered family men suddenly become bloodthirsty daredevils. Doctors risk life and limb to pass the pack. Long-suffering pastors cut others off in the turns. In our craziness, God's Spirit subtly helps us let our guards down and get comfortable with one another, even though some of us have never met.

After an hour or two of boyish fun, we head back to the meeting room in the hotel or break up into small groups. Everyone takes a few minutes to tell a little about himself. We typically recap information from earlier, but usually, someone risks going deeper.

One might say, "I'm here because I've really been playing church for a year now." Another might admit that his marriage is coming apart or his business is failing. God's Spirit is evident as each man lays aside bravado and becomes real.

HEADED FOR HIGHER GROUND

The next morning we eat breakfast at Pancake Pantry in Gatlinburg, make one last stop for snack food at a convenience market, and then head into the mountains. After parking the vehicles, we hit one of the trails leading to Mount LeConte Lodge near the summit. Usually, we travel the Alum Cave trail, a challenging four-hour hike, which winds through a forest, over a few creeks, up a series of steep foothills, around a sheer bluff or two, and through an evergreen forest before leading to the cabins on top.

As people stop to rest, take pictures, or adjust their packs along the way, we naturally break into small groups. We might talk more in-depth about what is going on in our lives, sing, recite Scriptures, or just be silent in God's creation.

Mount LeConte's facilities are primitive but inviting. There are a dining hall, a main hall with a dozen rocking chairs on the porch, and two rows of one-room cabins. With no electricity—we use kerosene lanterns for light— we feel like real mountain men (except for maybe our Gore-Tex® jackets and thermal-insulated boots).

After dinner, we assemble at a place called the Clifftop with an awesome view of the sunset. As the sky begins to change colors, we sing hymns and choruses. We call out verses that speak of God's greatness while the wind whips around us.

Soon the stars come out, and we make our way back down to the dining hall where several people tell about God's work in their lives. By this time, bonds are really established from man to man. We've spent twenty-four hours swapping stories, playing together, and marveling at nature.

WHEN A LIGHT COMES ON

On almost every trip, deep secrets come to light. Men talk honestly about intense struggles in their lives—addictions, problems in their families, grudges they hold, almost anything you can imagine. Many tears are shed during the meetings.

Men who thought they were totally alone, beaten down by some pain or problem, find others willing to love them through every situation. A few people confess they have been holding hurts inside for years, fearing that they would be rejected if they ever admitted they weren't as strong as they appeared to be. Prayers are offered, and prayers are answered.

Even though our time on Mount LeConte is a life-

changing experience for many men, we know we can't live on that mountaintop forever. In fact, we leave bright and early the next morning to go home.

Some people find the trip down the mountain much easier but not because gravity is on their side. Their hearts are lighter because God's love, expressed through His people, has broken chains of sin and lifted heavy burdens. I've learned to value the help of a close circle of friends.

A CLOSE CIRCLE OF FRIENDS

At times, I have acted like a temperamental artist or just a spoiled kid about situations in my life. I'm not above being prideful or arrogant or self-centered. That's why I have invited a close circle of friends to get in my face when they see I'm out of line. I don't recommend that you let people just take potshots at you, but I have truly experienced the benefits of people who have the freedom to challenge my thinking and ask me hard questions about life.

You need a few people like that too. Your life will be richer for forging a relationship with friends so committed to you they will not tolerate your getting away with sweeping dirt under the rug.

There's a flip side to this story too—the good stuff.

Just as Scripture says that we are to mourn with those who mourn, we get to rejoice with those who rejoice.

When my sister and brother-in-law had their first child a year or so ago, a whole army of family members welcomed her to the world.

We were meant to be joined at the heart to each other. We were meant for relationship with each other and with God.

Often, just the example of our parents and Christian friends can help us to live better lives.

THE WITNESS OF
FAMILY AND FRIENDS

I was blessed to grow up in a family where God came first and everyone was really committed to each other. I've said that I grew up wanting to be Opie Taylor from The Andy Griffith Show, *and in a way that's what my life was like. Kenova was not that much bigger than Mayberry. I had a dad who came to all of my ball games (he just happened to be the coach) and a mom who was like June Cleaver, cooking for everybody and every event. We went to church as a family. I know that very few people today have the kind of stability that I had growing up.*

Now that I'm a husband and a father I use the same guidelines that I saw modeled so well by my folks. "Husbands, love your wives, just as Christ also loved the church and gave Himself for her," it says in Ephesians 5:25.

When I think about how much love that is, my first reaction is to think that no one is up to that challenge.

If you've listened to any of my albums, you've probably heard at least one song I've written for my wife, Debbie. I can't imagine living without her. We balance each other, challenge each other, complement each other. When I'm blowing it with one of the kids, she delivers the right words of godly wisdom. When she's freaking out about something, I know how to lower her blood pressure and put everything back into perspective. Just as Wayne Kirkpatrick helped me say on the I'll Lead You Home album, she really is "the other side of me." God gave us each other to provide consolation, encouragement, and stability.

Over the years, Debbie and I have been honored to become friends with Billy and Ruth Graham. Watching how they relate to each other helps Deb and me grow as a couple. Because they have five kids just as we do and I'm on the road a lot as Dr. Graham is, Ruth Graham has been unbelievably gracious to offer Debbie support. Ruth's wisdom helps Deb just as having long talks with Dr. Graham has challenged me as a husband and a dad.

CHRIST'S SECRET PLAN

In His last opportunity to speak with the disciples before His arrest and crucifixion, Christ told them: "A new commandment I give to you, that you love one another; as I have loved you, that you also love one another. By this all will know that you are My disciples, if you have love for one another" (John 13:34–35).

Somewhere along the way, you may have heard somebody say that he or she wants to be a vessel for God's love. That makes it sound as if His love can be hoarded until it's convenient to let a little spill over onto someone else.

I think God has much more dynamic intentions for His love. I believe He wants each of us to be a conduit just as electricity passes through the wiring of a house where an outlet makes it possible to have light at any moment. Although I'm not there yet, I want to be so in touch with God that I could walk in a room and people would sense God's presence.

How does that sound to you? Insane? Unrealistic? Irresistible?

Not really. I've known people who are like this, people like Joe White at Kamp Kanakuk, a Christian camp in Missouri. I've learned to love my wife and kids better as I've seen him in action with his family. And I've watched how he gives 100 percent when it comes to influencing the kids who spend time at his camp.

He and his staff bring in some of the toughest inner-city kids you can imagine and absolutely melt their hearts by loving them into a relationship with Christ. He has pulled me aside and told their stories—this one's mom is a drug dealer, that little boy has witnessed seven murders, that girl waited all night for her dad to take her to the movies and her daddy never came. It is impossible to convey how passionate Joe is about communicating the gospel to the kids at Kanakuk. For him, that's what it means to love God with all his heart, soul, and mind.

Our relationships absolutely must reflect Christ's heart. Many people will never slide into the back row of a church or attend a Christian retreat or camp. They may not place themselves in an environment like the one I enjoyed at Mount LeConte. God's calling on our lives is to reach out to them, to take the beauty of His love to people everywhere we go. We weren't made to live alone.

PROMISES FOR VARIOUS RELATIONSHIPS

MARRIAGE

He who finds a wife finds a good thing,
And obtains favor from the LORD.

PROVERBS 18:22

And the LORD God said, "It is not good that man should be alone; I will make him a helper comparable to him."

GENESIS 2:18

Therefore a man shall leave his father and mother and be joined to his wife, and they shall become one flesh.

GENESIS 2:24

Who can find a virtuous wife?
For her worth is far above rubies.
The heart of her husband safely trusts her;
So he will have no lack of gain.
She does him good and not evil
All the days of her life.

PROVERBS 31:10–12

Therefore I desire that the younger widows marry, bear children, manage the house, give no opportunity to the adversary to speak reproachfully.

1 TIMOTHY 5:14

Now concerning the things of which you wrote to me: It is good for a man not to touch a woman. Nevertheless, because of sexual immorality, let each man have his own wife, and let each woman have her own husband. Let the husband render to his wife the affection due her, and likewise also the wife to her husband. The wife does not have authority over her own body, but the husband does. And likewise the husband does not have authority over his own body, but the wife does. Do not deprive one another except with consent for a time, that you may give yourselves to fasting and prayer; and come together again so that Satan does not tempt you because of your lack of self-control.

1 CORINTHIANS 7:1–5

Marriage is honorable among all, and the bed undefiled; but fornicators and adulterers God will judge.

HEBREWS 13:4

An excellent wife is the crown of her husband,
But she who causes shame is like rottenness in his
    bones.

PROVERBS 12:4

But even if she does depart, let her remain unmarried or be reconciled to her husband. And a husband is not to divorce his wife. But to the rest I, not the Lord, say: If any brother has a wife who does not believe, and she is willing to live with him, let him not divorce her.

1 CORINTHIANS 7:11–12

Charm is deceitful and beauty is passing,
But a woman who fears the LORD, she shall be
    praised.
Give her of the fruit of her hands,
And let her own works praise her in the gates.

PROVERBS 31:30–31

Your wife shall be like a fruitful vine
In the very heart of your house,
Your children like olive plants
All around your table.
Behold, thus shall the man be blessed
Who fears the LORD.
The LORD bless you out of Zion,
And may you see the good of Jerusalem
All the days of your life.
Yes, may you see your children's children.
Peace be upon Israel!

PSALM 128:3–6

You shall teach them to your children, speaking of them when you sit in your house, when you walk by the way, when you lie down, and when you rise up. And you shall write them on the doorposts of your house and on your gates, that your days and the days of your children may be multiplied in the land of which the LORD swore to your fathers to give them, like the days of the heavens above the earth.

DEUTERONOMY 11:19–21

Wives, likewise, be submissive to your own husbands, that even if some do not obey the word, they, without a word, may be won by the conduct of their wives.

1 PETER 3:1

Husbands, likewise, dwell with them with understanding, giving honor to the wife, as to the weaker vessel, and as being heirs together of the grace of life, that your prayers may not be hindered.

1 PETER 3:7

Hatred stirs up strife,
But love covers all sins.

PROVERBS 10:12

For this is the will of God, your sanctification: that you should abstain from sexual immorality; that each of you should know how to possess his own vessel in sanctification and honor, not in passion of lust, like the Gentiles who do not know God; that no one should take advantage of and defraud his brother in this matter, because the Lord is the avenger of all such, as we also forewarned you and testified.

1 Thessalonians 4:3–6

BUSINESS

Beloved, I pray that you may prosper in all things and be in health, just as your soul prospers.

3 John 1:2

And you shall remember the LORD your God, for it is He who gives you power to get wealth, that He may establish His covenant which He swore to your fathers, as it is this day.

Deuteronomy 8:18

Trust in the LORD with all your heart,
And lean not on your own understanding;
In all your ways acknowledge Him,
And He shall direct your paths.
Do not be wise in your own eyes;
Fear the LORD and depart from evil.
It will be health to your flesh,
And strength to your bones.
Honor the LORD with your possessions,
And with the firstfruits of all your increase;

So your barns will be filled with plenty,
And your vats will overflow with new wine.

PROVERBS 3:5–10

Commit your works to the LORD,
And your thoughts will be established.

PROVERBS 16:3

Through wisdom a house is built,
And by understanding it is established;
By knowledge the rooms are filled
With all precious and pleasant riches.

PROVERBS 24:3–4

If they obey and serve Him,
They shall spend their days in prosperity,
And their years in pleasures.

JOB 36:11

The LORD will command the blessing on you in
your storehouses and in all to which you set your
hand, and He will bless you in the land which the
LORD your God is giving you.

DEUTERONOMY 28:8

Masters, give your bondservants what is just and
fair, knowing that you also have a Master in
heaven.

COLOSSIANS 4:1

And the LORD will grant you plenty of goods, in the fruit of your body, in the increase of your livestock, and in the produce of your ground, in the land of which the LORD swore to your fathers to give you. The LORD will open to you His good treasure, the heavens, to give the rain to your land in its season, and to bless all the work of your hand. You shall lend to many nations, but you shall not borrow. And the LORD will make you the head and not the tail; you shall be above only, and not be beneath, if you heed the commandments of the LORD your God, which I command you today, and are careful to observe them.

DEUTERONOMY 28:11–13

But seek first the kingdom of God and His righteousness, and all these things shall be added to you.

MATTHEW 6:33

I go the way of all the earth; be strong, therefore, and prove yourself a man. And keep the charge of the LORD your God: to walk in His ways, to keep His statutes, His commandments, His judgments, and His testimonies, as it is written in the Law of Moses, that you may prosper in all that you do and wherever you turn.

1 KINGS 2:2–3

Then you will prosper, if you take care to fulfill the statutes and judgments with which the LORD charged Moses concerning Israel. Be strong and of good courage; do not fear nor be dismayed.

1 CHRONICLES 22:13

When you eat the labor of your hands,
You shall be happy, and it shall be well with you.

PSALM 128:2

Then you will lay your gold in the dust,
And the gold of Ophir among the stones of the
    brooks.
Yes, the Almighty will be your gold
And your precious silver.

JOB 22:24–25

Then He will give the rain for your seed
With which you sow the ground,
And bread of the increase of the earth;
It will be fat and plentiful.
In that day your cattle will feed
In large pastures.

ISAIAH 30:23

He also blesses them, and they multiply greatly;
And He does not let their cattle decrease.

PSALM 107:38

They shall build houses and inhabit them;
They shall plant vineyards and eat their fruit.
They shall not build and another inhabit;
They shall not plant and another eat;
For as the days of a tree, so shall be the days of My
    people,
And My elect shall long enjoy the work of their
    hands.
They shall not labor in vain,
Nor bring forth children for trouble;
For they shall be the descendants of the blessed of
    the LORD,
And their offspring with them.

ISAIAH 65:21–23

Wealth and riches will be in his house,
And his righteousness endures forever.

PSALM 112:3

Riches and honor are with me,
Enduring riches and righteousness.
My fruit is better than gold, yes, than fine gold,
And my revenue than choice silver.

PROVERBS 8:18–19

SOCIAL

You are the light of the world. A city that is set on a
hill cannot be hidden. Nor do they light a lamp
and put it under a basket, but on a lampstand, and

it gives light to all who are in the house. Let your light so shine before men, that they may see your good works and glorify your Father in heaven.

MATTHEW 5:14–16

Let love be without hypocrisy. Abhor what is evil. Cling to what is good. Be kindly affectionate to one another with brotherly love, in honor giving preference to one another; not lagging in diligence, fervent in spirit, serving the Lord; rejoicing in hope, patient in tribulation, continuing steadfastly in prayer; distributing to the needs of the saints, given to hospitality. Bless those who persecute you; bless and do not curse. Rejoice with those who rejoice, and weep with those who weep.

ROMANS 12:9–15

A new commandment I give to you, that you love one another; as I have loved you, that you also love one another. By this all will know that you are My disciples, if you have love for one another.

JOHN 13:34–35

For none of us lives to himself, and no one dies to himself. For if we live, we live to the Lord; and if we die, we die to the Lord. Therefore, whether we live or die, we are the Lord's.

ROMANS 14:7–8

Woe to him who builds his house by
    unrighteousness
And his chambers by injustice,
Who uses his neighbor's service without wages
And gives him nothing for his work.

JEREMIAH 22:13

You are the salt of the earth; but if the salt loses its
flavor, how shall it be seasoned? It is then good for
nothing but to be thrown out and trampled
underfoot by men.

MATTHEW 5:13

Therefore do not let your good be spoken of as
evil; for the kingdom of God is not eating and
drinking, but righteousness and peace and joy in
the Holy Spirit. For he who serves Christ in these
things is acceptable to God and approved by men.
Therefore let us pursue the things which make for
peace and the things by which one may edify
another. Do not destroy the work of God for the
sake of food. All things indeed are pure, but it is
evil for the man who eats with offense. It is good
neither to eat meat nor drink wine nor do anything
by which your brother stumbles or is offended or is
made weak.

ROMANS 14:16–21

You shall not cheat your neighbor, nor rob him.
The wages of him who is hired shall not remain
with you all night until morning.

LEVITICUS 19:13

Owe no one anything except to love one another,
for he who loves another has fulfilled the law. For
the commandments, "You shall not commit
adultery," "You shall not murder," "You shall not
steal," "You shall not bear false witness," "You shall
not covet," and if there is any other
commandment, are all summed up in this saying,
namely, "You shall love your neighbor as yourself."
Love does no harm to a neighbor; therefore love is
the fulfillment of the law.

ROMANS 13:8–10

Therefore, as the elect of God, holy and beloved,
put on tender mercies, kindness, humility,
meekness, longsuffering; bearing with one another,
and forgiving one another, if anyone has a
complaint against another; even as Christ forgave
you, so you also must do. But above all these things
put on love, which is the bond of perfection. And
let the peace of God rule in your hearts, to which
also you were called in one body; and be thankful.

COLOSSIANS 3:12–15

CHURCH

Simon Peter answered and said, "You are the Christ, the Son of the living God." Jesus answered and said to him, "Blessed are you, Simon Bar-Jonah, for flesh and blood has not revealed this to you, but My Father who is in heaven. And I also say to you that you are Peter, and on this rock I will build My church, and the gates of Hades shall not prevail against it. And I will give you the keys of the kingdom of heaven, and whatever you bind on earth will be bound in heaven, and whatever you loose on earth will be loosed in heaven."

MATTHEW 16:16–19

That in the dispensation of the fullness of the times He might gather together in one all things in Christ, both which are in heaven and which are on earth—in Him.

EPHESIANS 1:10

And He put all things under His feet, and gave Him to be head over all things to the church, which is His body, the fullness of Him who fills all in all.

EPHESIANS 1:22–23

But Jesus called them to Himself and said, "You know that the rulers of the Gentiles lord it over them, and those who are great exercise authority over them. Yet it shall not be so among you; but whoever desires to become great among you, let him be your servant."

MATTHEW 20:25–26

No longer do I call you servants, for a servant does not know what his master is doing; but I have called you friends, for all things that I heard from My Father I have made known to you. You did not choose Me, but I chose you and appointed you that you should go and bear fruit, and that your fruit should remain, that whatever you ask the Father in My name He may give you.

JOHN 15:15–16

These all continued with one accord in prayer and supplication, with the women and Mary the mother of Jesus, and with His brothers.

ACTS 1:14

When the Day of Pentecost had fully come, they were all with one accord in one place.

ACTS 2:1

For no one ever hated his own flesh, but nourishes and cherishes it, just as the Lord does the church. For we are members of His body, of His flesh and of His bones.

EPHESIANS 5:29–30

So continuing daily with one accord in the temple, and breaking bread from house to house, they ate their food with gladness and simplicity of heart, praising God and having favor with all the people. And the Lord added to the church daily those who were being saved.

ACTS 2:46–47

And a servant of the Lord must not quarrel but be gentle to all, able to teach, patient, in humility correcting those who are in opposition, if God perhaps will grant them repentance, so that they may know the truth, and that they may come to their senses and escape the snare of the devil, having been taken captive by him to do his will.

2 TIMOTHY 2:24–26

A new commandment I give to you, that you love one another; as I have loved you, that you also love one another.

JOHN 13:34

Then the churches throughout all Judea, Galilee, and Samaria had peace and were edified. And walking in the fear of the Lord and in the comfort of the Holy Spirit, they were multiplied.

ACTS 9:31

Now to Him who is able to do exceedingly abundantly above all that we ask or think, according to the power that works in us, to Him be glory in the church by Christ Jesus to all generations, forever and ever. Amen.

EPHESIANS 3:20–21

Let the word of Christ dwell in you richly in all wisdom, teaching and admonishing one another in psalms and hymns and spiritual songs, singing with grace in your hearts to the Lord. And whatever you do in word or deed, do all in the name of the Lord Jesus, giving thanks to God the Father through Him.

COLOSSIANS 3:16–17

GOVERNMENT

Therefore submit yourselves to every ordinance of man for the Lord's sake, whether to the king as supreme, or to governors, as to those who are sent by him for the punishment of evildoers and for the praise of those who do good. For this is the will of God, that by doing good you may put to silence the ignorance of foolish men.

1 PETER 2:13–15

Let every soul be subject to the governing authorities. For there is no authority except from God, and the authorities that exist are appointed by God. Therefore whoever resists the authority resists the ordinance of God, and those who resist will bring judgment on themselves. For rulers are not a terror to good works, but to evil. Do you want to be unafraid of the authority? Do what is good, and you will have praise from the same. For he is God's minister to you for good. But if you do evil, be afraid; for he does not bear the sword in vain; for he is God's minister, an avenger to execute wrath on him who practices evil. Therefore you must be subject, not only because of wrath but also for conscience' sake. For because of this you also pay taxes, for they are God's ministers attending continually to this very thing. Render therefore to all their due: taxes to whom taxes are due, customs to whom customs, fear to whom fear, honor to whom honor.

ROMANS 13:1–7

Remind them to be subject to rulers and authorities, to obey, to be ready for every good work, to speak evil of no one, to be peaceable, gentle, showing all humility to all men.

TITUS 3:1–2

It is an abomination for kings to commit wickedness,
For a throne is established by righteousness.

PROVERBS 16:12

Mercy and truth preserve the king,
And by lovingkindness he upholds his throne.

PROVERBS 20:28

The king who judges the poor with truth,
His throne will be established forever.

PROVERBS 29:14

This decision is by the decree of the watchers,
And the sentence by the word of the holy ones,
In order that the living may know
That the Most High rules in the kingdom of men,
Gives it to whomever He will,
And sets over it the lowest of men.

DANIEL 4:17

Then Samuel called the people together to the
LORD at Mizpah, and said to the children of
Israel, "Thus says the LORD God of Israel: 'I
brought up Israel out of Egypt, and delivered you
from the hand of the Egyptians and from the
hand of all kingdoms and from those who
oppressed you.' But you have today rejected your
God, who Himself saved you from all your
adversities and your tribulations; and you have
said to Him, 'No, set a king over us!' Now
therefore, present yourselves before the LORD by
your tribes and by your clans."

1 SAMUEL 10:17–19

Now therefore, here is the king whom you have
chosen and whom you have desired. And take note,
the LORD has set a king over you. If you fear the
LORD and serve Him and obey His voice, and do

not rebel against the commandment of the LORD, then both you and the king who reigns over you will continue following the LORD your God. However, if you do not obey the voice of the LORD, but rebel against the commandment of the LORD, then the hand of the LORD will be against you, as it was against your fathers.

1 SAMUEL 12:13–15

UNSAVED LOVED ONES

Even so it is not the will of your Father who is in heaven that one of these little ones should perish.

MATTHEW 18:14

The Lord is not slack concerning His promise, as some count slackness, but is longsuffering toward us, not willing that any should perish but that all should come to repentance.

2 PETER 3:9

Train up a child in the way he should go,
And when he is old he will not depart from it.

PROVERBS 22:6

Wives, likewise, be submissive to your own husbands, that even if some do not obey the word, they, without a word, may be won by the conduct of their wives, when they observe your chaste conduct accompanied by fear.

1 PETER 3:1–2

But even if you should suffer for righteousness'
sake, you are blessed. "And do not be afraid of their
threats, nor be troubled." But sanctify the Lord
God in your hearts, and always be ready to give a
defense to everyone who asks you a reason for the
hope that is in you, with meekness and fear; having
a good conscience, that when they defame you as
evildoers, those who revile your good conduct in
Christ may be ashamed.

1 PETER 3:14–16

So they said, "Believe on the Lord Jesus Christ, and
you will be saved, you and your household."

ACTS 16:31

Who will tell you words by which you and all your
household will be saved.

ACTS 11:14

And a woman who has a husband who does not
believe, if he is willing to live with her, let her not
divorce him. For the unbelieving husband is
sanctified by the wife, and the unbelieving wife is
sanctified by the husband; otherwise your children
would be unclean, but now they are holy. But if the
unbeliever departs, let him depart; a brother or a
sister is not under bondage in such cases. But God
has called us to peace. For how do you know, O
wife, whether you will save your husband? Or how

do you know, O husband, whether you will save your wife?

1 CORINTHIANS 7:13–16

You are the salt of the earth; but if the salt loses its flavor, how shall it be seasoned? It is then good for nothing but to be thrown out and trampled underfoot by men.

MATTHEW 5:13

You are the light of the world. A city that is set on a hill cannot be hidden. Nor do they light a lamp and put it under a basket, but on a lampstand, and it gives light to all who are in the house. Let your light so shine before men, that they may see your good works and glorify your Father in heaven.

MATTHEW 5:14–16

If anyone speaks, let him speak as the oracles of God. If anyone ministers, let him do it as with the ability which God supplies, that in all things God may be glorified through Jesus Christ, to whom belong the glory and the dominion forever and ever. Amen.

1 PETER 4:11

If you are reproached for the name of Christ, blessed are you, for the Spirit of glory and of God rests upon you. On their part He is blasphemed, but on your part He is glorified.

1 PETER 4:14

By this all will know that you are My disciples, if you have love for one another.

JOHN 13:35

THE ELDERLY

O God, You have taught me from my youth;
And to this day I declare Your wondrous works.
Now also when I am old and grayheaded,
O God, do not forsake me,
Until I declare Your strength to this generation,
Your power to everyone who is to come.

PSALM 71:17–18

With long life I will satisfy him,
And show him My salvation.

PSALM 91:16

Even to your old age, I am He,
And even to gray hairs I will carry you!
I have made, and I will bear;
Even I will carry, and will deliver you.

ISAIAH 46:4

The silver-haired head is a crown of glory,
If it is found in the way of righteousness.

PROVERBS 16:31

They shall still bear fruit in old age;
They shall be fresh and flourishing.

PSALM 92:14

The glory of young men is their strength,
And the splendor of old men is their gray head.

PROVERBS 20:29

For length of days and long life
And peace they will add to you.

PROVERBS 3:2

Length of days is in her right hand,
In her left hand riches and honor.

PROVERBS 3:16

Let your conduct be without covetousness; be
content with such things as you have. For He
Himself has said, "I will never leave you nor
forsake you."

HEBREWS 13:5

You shall walk in all the ways which the LORD your
God has commanded you, that you may live and
that it may be well with you, and that you may

prolong your days in the land which you shall possess.

DEUTERONOMY 5:33

That you may fear the LORD your God, to keep all His statutes and His commandments which I command you, you and your son and your grandson, all the days of your life, and that your days may be prolonged.

DEUTERONOMY 6:2

I have set the LORD always before me;
Because He is at my right hand I shall not be
   moved.

PSALM 16:8

You shall come to the grave at a full age,
As a sheaf of grain ripens in its season.

JOB 5:26

For by me your days will be multiplied,
And years of life will be added to you.

PROVERBS 9:11

Of Benjamin he said:
   "The beloved of the LORD shall dwell in safety
   by Him,
   Who shelters him all the day long;
   And he shall dwell between His shoulders."

DEUTERONOMY 33:12

The fear of the LORD prolongs days,
But the years of the wicked will be shortened.

PROVERBS 10:27

SATAN

And the God of peace will crush Satan under your feet shortly. The grace of our Lord Jesus Christ be with you. Amen.

ROMANS 16:20

Finally, my brethren, be strong in the Lord and in the power of His might. Put on the whole armor of God, that you may be able to stand against the wiles of the devil. For we do not wrestle against flesh and blood, but against principalities, against powers, against the rulers of the darkness of this age, against spiritual hosts of wickedness in the heavenly places.

EPHESIANS 6:10–12

Therefore submit to God. Resist the devil and he will flee from you.

JAMES 4:7

Be sober, be vigilant; because your adversary the devil walks about like a roaring lion, seeking whom he may devour. Resist him, steadfast in the faith, knowing that the same sufferings are experienced by your brotherhood in the world.

1 PETER 5:8–9

But we see Jesus, who was made a little lower than the angels, for the suffering of death crowned with glory and honor, that He, by the grace of God, might taste death for everyone.

HEBREWS 2:9

Inasmuch then as the children have partaken of flesh and blood, He Himself likewise shared in the same, that through death He might destroy him who had the power of death, that is, the devil, and release those who through fear of death were all their lifetime subject to bondage.

HEBREWS 2:14–15

Therefore take up the whole armor of God, that you may be able to withstand in the evil day, and having done all, to stand. Stand therefore, having girded your waist with truth, having put on the breastplate of righteousness, and having shod your feet with the preparation of the gospel of peace; above all, taking the shield of faith with which you will be able to quench all the fiery darts of the wicked one. And take the helmet of salvation, and the sword of the Spirit, which is the word of God; praying always with all prayer and supplication in the Spirit, being watchful to this end with all perseverance and supplication for all the saints.

EPHESIANS 6:13–18

Beloved, do not believe every spirit, but test the spirits, whether they are of God; because many false prophets have gone out into the world. By this you know the Spirit of God: Every spirit that confesses that Jesus Christ has come in the flesh is of God, and every spirit that does not confess that Jesus Christ has come in the flesh is not of God. And this is the spirit of the Antichrist, which you have heard was coming, and is now already in the world. You are of God, little children, and have overcome them, because He who is in you is greater than he who is in the world.

1 JOHN 4:1–4

And they overcame him by the blood of the Lamb and by the word of their testimony, and they did not love their lives to the death.

REVELATION 12:11

How you are fallen from heaven,
O Lucifer, son of the morning!
How you are cut down to the ground,
You who weakened the nations!
For you have said in your heart:
"I will ascend into heaven,
I will exalt my throne above the stars of God;
I will also sit on the mount of the congregation
On the farthest sides of the north;
I will ascend above the heights of the clouds,
I will be like the Most High."

Yet you shall be brought down to Sheol,
To the lowest depths of the Pit.

ISAIAH 14:12–15

He who sins is of the devil, for the devil has sinned
from the beginning. For this purpose the Son of
God was manifested, that He might destroy the
works of the devil.

1 JOHN 3:8

For though we walk in the flesh, we do not war
according to the flesh. For the weapons of our
warfare are not carnal but mighty in God for
pulling down strongholds, casting down arguments
and every high thing that exalts itself against the
knowledge of God, bringing every thought into
captivity to the obedience of Christ.

2 CORINTHIANS 10:3–5

But if I cast out demons by the Spirit of God,
surely the kingdom of God has come upon you. Or
how can one enter a strong man's house and
plunder his goods, unless he first binds the strong
man? And then he will plunder his house.

MATTHEW 12:28–29

Then the seventy returned with joy, saying, "Lord,
even the demons are subject to us in Your name."
And He said to them, "I saw Satan fall like
lightning from heaven. Behold, I give you the

authority to trample on serpents and scorpions, and over all the power of the enemy, and nothing shall by any means hurt you."

LUKE 10:17–19

And these signs will follow those who believe: In My name they will cast out demons; they will speak with new tongues; they will take up serpents; and if they drink anything deadly, it will by no means hurt them; they will lay hands on the sick, and they will recover.

MARK 16:17–18

And then the lawless one will be revealed, whom the Lord will consume with the breath of His mouth and destroy with the brightness of His coming.

2 THESSALONIANS 2:8

PROMISES FOR AN
ETERNAL FUTURE

I f you have listened to the album My Utmost for His Highest: The Covenant, *you've heard a song that David Mullen and I wrote that paints a picture of the future. Entitled "Someday (Set the Children Free)," the lyrics speak of how God will transform the lives that we know into what we long for them to be.*

We get glimpses of that every now and then on this earth, but those moments are nothing compared to what awaits us in heaven. The greatest source for images is found in the book of Revelation. If you've ever read it, you probably found things that just boggled your mind: the coming of the Antichrist, the mark of the Beast, a dragon, supernatural horsemen, and ultimately, Christ's promise of His return.

You're probably thinking, Smitty, why on earth would anybody want to read all that confusing stuff?

Yet Revelation 1:3 states, "Blessed is he who reads and those who hear the words of this prophecy, and keep those things which are written in it; for the time is near." Even though much of it is hard to understand, God promises a blessing just in reading Revelation and taking it to heart.

Several times our church read the entire book aloud as a special worship program. The effect was absolutely powerful. A couple of times I worked with a group of musicians to provide a live sound track that punctuated the text. As a group of dramatists read each section, we improvised musical accents.

When they spoke of battles in heaven, there were thundering trumpets and crashing cymbals. When they read about people bowing before God, we played a reverent, understated melody. In those twenty-two chapters, we used an unbelievably wide range of musical dynamics. By the time we reached the "Come, Lord Jesus!" section that closes the book, we felt a strong anticipation of what God will do one day.

Even after experiencing this program several times, I

still don't understand all that is written in the book. But this I do know: Christ will return just as He said He will. Maybe it will be today or a hundred years from now. No one knows. The point is to be ready to meet Him, just as a bride anticipates walking down the aisle to be married to her groom.

UNTIL THAT DAY

Until Christ returns for us, we live in expectation that someday things will be far better than we have experienced. I find encouragement when I read this promise for believers from chapter 7: "They shall never hunger anymore nor thirst anymore; the sun shall not strike them, nor any heat; for the Lamb who is in the midst of the throne will shepherd them and lead them to living fountains of waters. And God will wipe away every tear from their eyes" (vv. 16–17).

There's also great comfort as we look to a future in heaven where "there shall be no more death, nor sorrow, nor crying. There shall be no more pain, for the former things have passed away" (21:4). He even said, "Behold, I make all things new" (21:5).

Wheelchairs and pacemakers will be obsolete. The scars of abuse will be gone. Our darkest secrets will be absorbed by perfect light. There won't be any dividing lines *between the haves and the have-nots, between denominations or races.*

CLOSING TIME

My prayer for you when you graduate and write the next chapter of your life is that "Christ may dwell in your [heart] through faith; that you, being rooted and grounded in love, may be able to comprehend with all the saints what is the width and length and depth and height" of God's love (Eph. 3:17–18).

Just as I told those eighty-three graduates at Ceredo-Kenova High School in 1991, I believe that God has big plans for you. Will you trust Him to bring those things into focus? Maybe you'll become the next Billy Graham or the doctor who discovers a cure for cancer. Maybe you'll turn the world upside down in your own unique way. But maybe His big plan for you takes a different form. Maybe you'll become the kind of parent that all the kids in your neighborhood wish they had. Maybe you will so love your spouse that others will look to you as an example. Maybe you will become a mature and trustworthy friend, respected for your godly counsel and generous spirit. In doing so, you demonstrate what it means to love your God with all your heart, mind, and soul, and to love those around you as yourself.

As I charged you at the beginning, I come back again to say, "Delight yourself also in the LORD, and He shall give you the desires of your heart" (Ps. 37:4).

Until Someday arrives, be strong in His might.

PROMISES FOR AN ETERNAL FUTURE

A GLORIOUS RESURRECTION

Jesus said to her, "I am the resurrection and the life. He who believes in Me, though he may die, he shall live."

JOHN 11:25

And many of those who sleep in the dust of the earth shall awake,
Some to everlasting life,
Some to shame and everlasting contempt.

DANIEL 12:2

Do not marvel at this; for the hour is coming in which all who are in the graves will hear His voice and come forth—those who have done good, to the

resurrection of life, and those who have done evil,
to the resurrection of condemnation.

JOHN 5:28–29

Your dead shall live;
Together with my dead body they shall arise.
Awake and sing, you who dwell in dust;
For your dew is like the dew of herbs,
And the earth shall cast out the dead.

ISAIAH 26:19

For since by man came death, by Man also came
the resurrection of the dead.

1 CORINTHIANS 15:21

But those who are counted worthy to attain that
age, and the resurrection from the dead, neither
marry nor are given in marriage; nor can they die
anymore, for they are equal to the angels and are
sons of God, being sons of the resurrection.

LUKE 20:35–36

But if the Spirit of Him who raised Jesus from the
dead dwells in you, He who raised Christ from the
dead will also give life to your mortal bodies
through His Spirit who dwells in you.

ROMANS 8:11

So also is the resurrection of the dead. The body is
sown in corruption, it is raised in incorruption. It is

sown in dishonor, it is raised in glory. It is sown in weakness, it is raised in power. It is sown a natural body, it is raised a spiritual body. There is a natural body, and there is a spiritual body.

1 CORINTHIANS 15:42–44

Knowing that He who raised up the Lord Jesus will also raise us up with Jesus, and will present us with you.

2 CORINTHIANS 4:14

Who will transform our lowly body that it may be conformed to His glorious body, according to the working by which He is able even to subdue all things to Himself.

PHILIPPIANS 3:21

For if we believe that Jesus died and rose again, even so God will bring with Him those who sleep in Jesus. For this we say to you by the word of the Lord, that we who are alive and remain until the coming of the Lord will by no means precede those who are asleep. For the Lord Himself will descend from heaven with a shout, with the voice of an archangel, and with the trumpet of God. And the dead in Christ will rise first. Then we who are alive and remain shall be caught up together with them in the clouds to meet the Lord in the air. And thus we shall always be with the Lord.

1 THESSALONIANS 4:14–17

ETERNAL LIFE

And this is the promise that He has promised us—
eternal life.

1 JOHN 2:25

Most assuredly, I say to you, he who believes in Me
has everlasting life.

JOHN 6:47

Jesus said to her, "I am the resurrection and the life.
He who believes in Me, though he may die, he shall
live. And whoever lives and believes in Me shall
never die. Do you believe this?"

JOHN 11:25–26

But now having been set free from sin, and having
become slaves of God, you have your fruit to
holiness, and the end, everlasting life. For the wages
of sin is death, but the gift of God is eternal life in
Christ Jesus our Lord.

ROMANS 6:22–23

My sheep hear My voice, and I know them, and
they follow Me. And I give them eternal life, and
they shall never perish; neither shall anyone snatch
them out of My hand.

JOHN 10:27–28

Whoever eats My flesh and drinks My blood has eternal life, and I will raise him up at the last day.

JOHN 6:54

And these will go away into everlasting punishment, but the righteous into eternal life.

MATTHEW 25:46

Nor can they die anymore, for they are equal to the angels and are sons of God, being sons of the resurrection.

LUKE 20:36

In hope of eternal life which God, who cannot lie, promised before time began.

TITUS 1:2

And this is the testimony: that God has given us eternal life, and this life is in His Son.

1 JOHN 5:11

These things I have written to you who believe in the name of the Son of God, that you may know that you have eternal life, and that you may continue to believe in the name of the Son of God.

1 JOHN 5:13

For God so loved the world that He gave His only begotten Son, that whoever believes in Him should not perish but have everlasting life.

JOHN 3:16

But whoever drinks of the water that I shall give him will never thirst. But the water that I shall give him will become in him a fountain of water springing up into everlasting life.

JOHN 4:14

Most assuredly, I say to you, he who hears My word and believes in Him who sent Me has everlasting life, and shall not come into judgment, but has passed from death into life.

JOHN 5:24

Do not labor for the food which perishes, but for the food which endures to everlasting life, which the Son of Man will give you, because God the Father has set His seal on Him.

JOHN 6:27

As You have given Him authority over all flesh, that He should give eternal life to as many as You have given Him.

JOHN 17:2

That having been justified by His grace we should become heirs according to the hope of eternal life.

TITUS 3:7

And we know that the Son of God has come and has given us an understanding, that we may know Him who is true; and we are in Him who is true, in His Son Jesus Christ. This is the true God and eternal life.

1 JOHN 5:20

PLAN OF SALVATION

You Are a Sinner . . .
As it is written:
"There is none righteous, no, not one."

ROMANS 3:10

There Is a Price to Be Paid for Sin . . .
For all have sinned and fall short of the glory of God.

ROMANS 3:23

Need to Repent . . .
But go and learn what this means: "I desire mercy and not sacrifice." For I did not come to call the righteous, but sinners, to repentance.

MATTHEW 9:13

I tell you, no; but unless you repent you will all likewise perish.

LUKE 13:3

God Loves You . . .
For God so loved the world that He gave His only begotten Son, that whoever believes in Him should not perish but have everlasting life.

JOHN 3:16

Christ Died for You and Wants to Save You . . .
For the wages of sin is death, but the gift of God is eternal life in Christ Jesus our Lord.

ROMANS 6:23

But God demonstrates His own love toward us, in that while we were still sinners, Christ died for us.

ROMANS 5:8

Christ Will Save You Now . . .
That if you confess with your mouth the Lord Jesus and believe in your heart that God has raised Him from the dead, you will be saved. For with the heart one believes unto righteousness, and with the mouth confession is made unto salvation.

ROMANS 10:9–10

Whoever calls on the name of the LORD shall be saved.

ROMANS 10:13

You Can Know That You Are Saved . . .
He who believes in the Son of God has the witness
in himself; he who does not believe God has made
Him a liar, because he has not believed the
testimony that God has given of His Son. And this
is the testimony: that God has given us eternal life,
and this life is in His Son. He who has the Son has
life; he who does not have the Son of God does not
have life. These things I have written to you who
believe in the name of the Son of God, that you
may know that you have eternal life, and that you
may continue to believe in the name of the Son of
God.

1 JOHN 5:10–13

May the Lord Continue To Draw you Closer To Him In An Awesome Way!

Your Friend,

[signature]

Autographs

Autographs